Henry Weyland Chetwynd

Mrs. Dorriman

Vol. II

Henry Weyland Chetwynd

Mrs. Dorriman
Vol. II

ISBN/EAN: 9783337041021

Printed in Europe, USA, Canada, Australia, Japan

Cover: Foto ©ninafisch / pixelio.de

More available books at **www.hansebooks.com**

MRS. DORRIMAN.

A Novel.

BY THE

HON. MRS. HENRY W. CHETWYND,

AUTHOR OF
"LIFE IN A GERMAN VILLAGE," "THE DUTCH COUSIN,"
"A MARCH VIOLET," "BEES AND BUTTERFLIES,"
ETC., ETC.

IN THREE VOLUMES.

VOL. II.

LONDON: CHAPMAN AND HALL
LIMITED
1886

WESTMINSTER:
PRINTED BY NICHOLS AND SONS,
25, PARLIAMENT STREET.

MRS. DORRIMAN.

CHAPTER I.

Man proposes . . . and wives sometimes interfere.

John went with the single and innocent object of conveying his master's wishes to Mr. Macrae. He found, however, that there were two sides to this as to all other questions.

Mr. Macrae was a portly, good-humoured man, who suffered from some perplexity as to the reason why his waistcoats had taken to hitching themselves up in front; waistcoats being, he supposed, made on different principles in these days. When he was younger, waistcoats had not this evil habit. The cut probably was different. His first action on being summoned was to pull down his waistcoat, his next to brush some imaginary crumbs off his coat-sleeves, and then to hold his head up and march off. But fate—and his wife—interposed. Mrs. Macrae was a slight woman, who was kindly and good-natured, but who had a keen eye to her own interests, and, who being more able than her husband to see those two sides of a question, had a slight contempt for his intellectual powers.

"If Sir Albert wants a little conversation I'll go myself," she said, with alacrity; "especially as Mr. Macrae cannot leave the bar at the busiest time of the day."

"But you'll do at the bar as well as myself," said her husband, unguardedly, preparing to go and yet not quite able to assert himself so decidedly.

"As well as yourself!" she returned, with strong contempt. "I'll do as well and better than you in both ways. Sir Albert probably wishes to speak about his diet, and what do you know about that?"

Mr. Macrae looked at John, who said, blandly, "I am sure master would be glad to see you, Mrs. Macrae, but I was to be sure and say, not if you was busy."

Mr. Macrae let things alone. He was quite able to perceive the great inconsistency of his wife's proceedings. How often did she not say to him that he was of no use, and she would be better without him, and yet now he could not be spared from the bar for even a few moments. He contented himself, however, by muttering a good deal of treason against the sex generally, and his wife in particular; and then he turned to the contemplation of the street and pier; watched the gambols of two dogs, and the unlading of a cart, and allowed his waistcoat to wrinkle up undisturbed.

John explained the situation in a hurried speech to his master, and, having left him comfortably disposed of for the time, went out also on the pier to look about him.

Mrs. Macrae looked at the young man with all the interest in him natural to her as his hostess, and a woman full of kindly sympathies. His strong constitution was pulling him through, but there was weakness and helplessness enough left, to appeal to all the kindest part of her nature.

"I am afraid I give a great deal of trouble, Mrs. Macrae," he began, in soft low rich tones — tones that would go far in his favour anywhere, she thought.

"Oh, never think of the trouble, sir. We are paid for taking trouble," she answered, hastily, an innate refinement making her anxious to lessen his sense of obligation.

"Ah! but you are not paid for taking it cheerfully. My servant says every one has been so kind and ready to help. You must allow me to feel obliged, and let me thank you."

"I am sure you are welcome, sir. How did it happen? it was a terrible accident. If it does not tire you to talk about it all, I should like to know."

" I am tired of silence," he said, pleasantly, " but if you would sit down, Mrs. Macrae, it would be very good of you. Seeing you stand gives me a feeling of fatigue."

Mrs. Macrae obeyed and drew a chair near, upon which she placed herself in a most uncomfortable attitude.

" There is little to tell," he said, after a moment's pause. " I went too near the edge of a disused quarry, I think, or the rains had undermined the ground I was on; at any rate, I took a step too near a part standing treacherously forward, and fell a good height, taking a quantity of loose stones and gravel with me. Then I remember nothing else."

" And I dare say you lay a long time before your man found you, sir. Well, it might have been worse, they might not have found you so soon."

" Oh, a young lady saw me first, and she got assistance."

A young lady! Mrs. Macrae pricked up her ears at this. Why, it was going to be a romance, she thought. "A young lady!" she said, aloud; "there are none so many here, sir. Do you know her name, sir; was it one you know?"

"I think I know her name," he answered, and he opened the little book lying beside him, and held it towards her. "Do you know her? where does she live?"

"Grace Rivers!" exclaimed Mrs. Macrae. "Why, those young ladies have been living here for some weeks; they are here now with their aunt; they are just going away. And how did you get that book?"

"She left it I suppose when she ran to call for help. My servant found it, and thought it was mine, and he brought it here."

"Well, it is a providential thing some one was by, you might have been killed, sir, and died with no one there. Miss Grace Rivers. Yes, yes. It is her, though Miss Margaret's the one that is aye rambling."

"When I am a little better I should like to see Miss Grace Rivers," said Sir Albert, with some hesitation, "to thank her; do you know where she lives?"

"Indeed, I do not, sir, when she is at home; but she and her sister are here just now."

"Here!" he exclaimed. "Do you mean in this house?"

"Yes, here, sir, and there's no need to excite yourself; they are here with a quiet nice lady, not a real aunt, but some way kin to them, and they're all going away soon."

"Oh, they are going away?" and Sir Albert felt unaccountably disappointed.

"Well, sir, they came for a few weeks, and they liked the place and liked the cooking and felt comfortable, and they stayed on."

"I am sure I do not wonder," said Sir Albert, politely, "if you make them as comfortable as you do me."

"Hoot, sir, and you that has aye slops. How can ye tell?" and Mrs. Macrae laughed comfortably; she was beginning to feel at her ease with him.

"Ah, slops—are slops," he said, with a little grimace, "but there is a right and a wrong way of sending them up. I still remember being ill at school, and the greasy broth and cold gruel—*cold* gruel!"

"And may be a deal paid for you there; well, I do not believe in schools for my part."

"Now your beef tea is good, though I am getting tired of it; and has the doctor never spoken to you about my moving? I am pining to get out."

"Ech, sir, and you all smashed—you are wonderful, and so cheerful."

"Am I cheerful? I am afraid you see your own reflection, Mrs. Macrae. I feel dull enough now I am out of pain. But I am very thankful," he added, in a more serious tone.

"I am sure, sir, we are all thankful too. It would have been a sair pity if you had come here a corpse, and that is bad for an hotel at any time too."

At that moment John entered and announced the doctor.

"I am earlier than usual, Sir Albert. I have to go some way off, but I wanted to see you first."

"Thanks! I am getting well fast."

"And wishing to go out," put in Mrs. Macrae, hoping to see the doctor's face express disapprobation and corroborate her oldfashioned idea of fresh air being bad for all cases of sickness.

"Of course, as soon as the moving does not pain you, you have severe bruises to recover from still—but fresh air. Yes, get out as soon as you can—lying here your spirits may go down. Yes, get out as soon as ever you can."

Sir Albert gave a triumphant smile to Mrs. Macrae, who rose and left them, much exercised in her mind about these new-fangled ways.

Thus it happened that soon a bath-chair was conveying Sir Albert along the level road by the sea, and that Mrs. Dorriman and Grace thus met him.

"Miss Grace Rivers and her aunt, Sir Albert," said John, hurriedly, as he saw them coming, and he was sent by his master to beg them to come and speak to him.

When they came nearer Sir Albert was conscious of a great and overwhelming disappointment. He must have dreamed of the expression in the girl's face, even the colour of her eyes. This face was like and yet unlike, and the cold steel-blue eyes, and the little self-satisfied expression, repelled him and made his proffered thanks an effort, all the time hating himself for being so ungrateful.

He apologised to Mrs. Dorriman for having ventured to detain her, but he was so anxious to express to Miss Rivers, Miss Grace Rivers, all he felt.

"Oh! I had nothing to do with it. It was my sister, it was Margaret," Grace said hurriedly.

"Yes," said Mrs. Dorriman, "poor Margaret came home quite ill from the fright and shock."

"I'll—I am so grieved," began Sir Albert.

"She is all right now," said Grace, quickly. "After all she was not able to help you."

"You do not know how she helped me,' said Sir Albert, quietly. "But for her courage in staying and bathing my face—even moving me—I might have died. I do hope I shall have an opportunity of seeing her and expressing my thanks in person."

"Of course you shall," said Grace abruptly, impatient of the subject, one in which she played no part.

Mrs. Dorriman felt interested in the helpless figure, and the pallor which spoke of much suffering—she would fain have lingered, but Grace hurried her on.

"I am so disappointed," exclaimed the young lady, "Sir Albert is grave, and not at all good-looking, so pale and cadaverous."

"It is not wonderful, having had such a terrible accident, my dear. I think he has such a fine face. I am sure his eyes are wonderful, there is patience written on his face."

"And he is grateful to Margaret, which is the only reason you are interested in him," said Grace, pettishly. "It is always Margaret."

Mrs. Dorriman said no more. When Grace took this tone she exercised a gift she possessed—a gift of greatest value—the golden gift of silence.

It was not many days after this, Margaret, who had been disturbed and anxious because of a scene between Mr. Sandford and Grace, had gone for the relief of quiet and fresh air along the sea-side. All around her lay the hush of evening, when all have rest. The sun was low and lighted up the western sky with a soft glow of golden colour, showing himself only behind high-fleeting clouds which but partly only veiled his glory. Every ripple on the sea caught a quivering touch of light, all the great hills took softening shadows, all inequalities seemed brought into one harmonious whole, as a fine soul will sometimes blend inconsistencies till they cease to strike one as incongruous. The light fell softly upon Margaret's face, and the little ruffle upon her brow, the sign of disturbance, was smoothed out.

In the midst of such a scene she felt that her irritation had been unworthy—how could she allow herself to feel things so much? She tried to set before herself Mr. Sandford's deeds of kindness, but she failed. She had a strong sense of justice, and it was unjust to heap obligations upon them upon the one hand, and make those obligations hateful on the other. What could she do to help Grace? How act so that she might in some way be saved from a life she hated, and out of which no good came to her.

She had another and a deeper trouble to bear. Mr. Sandford had never wished *her* to be particularly friendly, or even civil, to Mr. Drayton; but that uncongenial man had arrived that day, and Mr. Sandford had changed in his views. He had insisted upon Margaret's remaining to talk, and had shown great temper when she did so with evident reluctance; and this was a terrible trouble to her.

Was there nothing that she and Grace could do alone? was there no way of making a little home for themselves? She possessed no accomplishments, and though Grace was so very clever, and every one admired her performances, they had often lately tried selling something, and had failed.

If she went out as a governess she would not help Grace. They had so little, what could they do? What could she do? She imagined that it was the life that was hurting Grace, and that more favourable circumstances would raise her tone of mind, and this made all harder to bear.

She often thought with a real pang that Grace had thought her marriage to Mr. Drayton possible. Then she blamed herself for attaching too much importance to what was said in a moment of depression and misery.

She was losing herself in these thoughts, conceived of a passionate longing for something to help her, praying, as she often did, to be shown her way, and for patience, and, with her eyes fixed upon the light and her thoughts with God, she went on her way, and so Sir Albert Gerald met her once again.

Lying back in his bath-chair, he had been looking at the soft loveliness around him, thinking that such a sunset had more poetry and more beauty than the blaze of gold and crimson which, as a rule, presented itself when the sunset was not softened and veiled by clouds; and sharply defined against the evening sky he had seen a figure full of quiet grace, and before she drew near he recognised her, and thrilled with the recollection of the prayer she had breathed beside him.

There was no consciousness or shyness in her manner. She was glad to see him better, glad to meet him, and she put her hand into his outstretched towards her, with a feeling of relief and gladness. It would have been terrible had this powerful frame, this youth and strength, been crushed. His eyes rested upon her with intense satisfaction, he noted the straightforward open gaze, and the lovely smile that brought colour into her face. He had not dreamed it—she was lovely!

"I am so glad to see you out. You will soon get well," she said, and he thought her voice was as lovely as her face.

"You must let me thank you," he said earnestly. "You were so good and so brave. Most girls would have been too much frightened to help. Some would have fainted."

"I think not," she said, gravely, reddening a little under his earnest gaze. "I was too anxious to be of use to feel afraid. I think others would also have been anxious—others might have done more."

"Oh, no!" he said; "I am glad to have to be grateful to you. I have thought so much about it. I have so wished to know you."

"You have seen Mrs. Dorriman—you have

seen Grace, my sister, I mean," correcting herself.

"Yes; her name was in the book you had. I thought it belonged to you."

"Mine is a very common name—Margaret."

"I know. I think it is a beautiful name; it is my mother's name."

"Your mother has been, she must have been, very unhappy."

"Yes, but we only told her when I was getting better—poor mother! she cannot leave her sofa. She is carried everywhere.

"How sad!"

"Yes, it is terrible for her, and she has been to me father and mother, and brother and sister, since I am an only child."

"It must be so sad not to have a sister," said Margaret, softly. "It must be like not having the whole of oneself."

"And yet sometimes sisters do not get on," said Sir Albert, smiling, and thinking of episodes in his family history that pointed to a very different state of things.

Talking still, they turned at the end of the path, the road beyond being too rough for Sir Albert in his present condition; the faithful John pushed the chair back again, accommodating its pace to the footsteps of the girl who walked beside it. What is the subtle influence that makes one feel as though to one person all may be confided, and to another as though a visible barrier rises between you? It is not only sympathy, for sympathy comes when full appreciation for a common object is discovered, when the same bias of the mind is found in each; but the appreciation must first be known. It is something more—it is apart from love between man and woman (though love on one side or another frequently follows it); it is an unknown force compelling us to frankness, filling us with a sudden liking which we cannot reason about, and do not find ourselves able to account for.

Mr. Sandford, occupied by trying to mould Mr. Drayton to his wishes, prepared to carry his plans out at any sacrifice, little imagined that a sudden obstacle was rising in a quarter he never dreamed of,—like most of us, conscious of our hopes and wishes only, and never taking into account for one moment the many combinations against us.

This first meeting between two drawn together in the beginning by an hour of pain and anxiety, was naturally not the last. Margaret, sometimes with the others, sometimes with Grace, at times alone, met Sir Albert Gerald every day. Acquaintance with him did her good; his larger views were often opposed to her narrower experience, and in argument her prejudices and preconceived opinions gave way. She was truthful to herself as to others, and she was forced to allow the shallowness of her ground.

Upon his side there was a never-ending delight in the absolute freshness of her mind. Old ideas received a new beauty from her way of seeing them, and he was often startled by the poetry of a thought new to him.

The drawback to this pleasant acquaintance

was the sense of its finality. They did not know from day to day that Mr. Sandford might not put a stop to it by taking the whole party home.

Sir Albert, still a little weak from his severe accident, never paused to question himself where this delightful companionship was leading him. He only knew that in *her* presence he seemed to live. She drew out his noblest, highest, and best feelings. She was to him a guiding star; he loved her passionately, and he respected her as the purest and most perfect of God's creatures. There were in these few days none of those short partings which serve to teach the real nature of a similar feeling in most cases. There was that sense of impending parting possible, but far off, which is so different from an announced fact; there was nothing to shake them into consciousness.

They grew silent now when they were together, conscious of that full unison of thought that requires no outward expression—a glance, a look told all.

The trial to her was terrible just now, since she could say nothing, and Mr. Sandford gave the man she had begun to hate (Mr. Drayton) every opportunity of being with her; insisting upon her receiving his attentions, more dreadful to her now than ever.

She appealed to her uncle in private against this persecution—in vain. He knew now, though Mr. Drayton never put it into words, that the price of his own safety was—Margaret.

In his solitary moments he ground his teeth with rage—not because of her, poor child! but because he had unwittingly put himself into this position. He promised Mr. Drayton that he would use his influence, but he warned him that if he spoke now, when Margaret was full of repulsion for him, all hope would be at an end. "She has so high a spirit, that if she were driven to it she would go away."

Mr. Drayton laughed. "Fancy you owning yourself unable to cope with any young lady."

Mr. Sandford started from his chair, there

were many moments during their intercourse when the whole fabric he had raised seemed likely to fall; there were many days when he could hardly act his part—when remorse confronted him, seeing what the man was made of to whom he wished to consign Margaret.

Had Grace known then what she only learned afterwards!

She drove Mr. Sandford to distraction, she was so fitful, so impertinent, and so openly regardless of any expressed wish of his.

Then he grew violent, and Margaret was miserable.

It was after heavy rain; the sullen clouds had not yet begun to clear, and there was a grey, dull, leaden look upon the reflecting waves. Everything had combined to make poor Margaret miserable. Mr. Sandford had stormed, and there had been a scene before Mr. Drayton. Grace had been in the wrong, and this was an additional sorrow. Then Mr. Drayton had taken advantage of the family jar to pose as Margaret's defender, and afterwards Grace had spoken bitterly. Why could Margaret not accept this man (who had not Mr. Sandford's temper), and make a home for them both?

Distracted, wretched, her heart oppressed by the burden placed upon it by others—poor Margaret sped along the road where she had been when Sir Albert had fallen. She could not meet him then—she could not bear him to see her misery. She instinctively felt it might be an appeal to him, and he was her friend, she could not tax his friendship. Then suddenly she saw him for the first time walking.

"Great ideas meet," he called out, as he saw her coming. "I wanted to see the place that made us known to each other." Then, as she came closer he saw the traces of tears, the troubled look, and the small mouth was quivering. He stopped short; the sight of her distress showed him what she was to him. "Darling!" he said, softly; and then with a great effort he drove back the words rushing to his lips.

She heard him, however, and a look of perfect happiness flashed into her face.

He saw her turn towards him, surprised at his silence. He did not know she had heard that word.

He broke silence after a moment or two, forcing himself to speak calmly—while his heart was beating violently. "Are you surprised to see me walking again?" he said, with a faint attempt at a smile. "I can walk without pain, and I am not tired." She did not answer, she was too much overwhelmed by the sudden emotion of his betrayal of that one word, and the forced calm afterwards. What did it mean? Had she mistaken him? A perfect quiver of fear, a sudden sense of having by a look answered too readily something he had not said—or had said by accident —filled her with dismay.

He read her thought, and he could not help her. He bit his lip angrily. He had given his mother his solemn word of honour that never would he tell his love to any one till he had told her first of his intention; and it seemed to him in the great anguish of that moment that only now, only at that moment, did the truth come to him. They stood side by side looking out upon the sea, she dazed with the misery of having misunderstood; he thinking how he might show her that there was a reason for his silence, without breaking his word of honour. "Margaret," he said, and his voice dwelt lovingly upon her name, "We are—friends, and we may trust each other. I cannot say all—I am not free. Will you trust me?"

Her heart seemed to die within her. She of course did not understand him, poor child. Those words, *I am not free* should have ended "to speak just now;" but in moments of great agitation things are not always made clear.

She thought he was telling her, for her sake perhaps, that he was not free, that they could only be friends.

She turned towards him pale to her lips. "I understand," she said faintly, "we can be friends."

She had struggled for self-command; she was afraid of saying more, but he must let her know that he had something more to tell her—he was turning towards her to speak when she suddenly moved away from him with a gesture of farewell, and he was too feeble to follow her swiftly.

All along the road home her heart was throbbing with pain. She did not understand that in so leaving him she was betraying how deeply her affections were engaged.

He looked after her dismayed at first, and then the happy conviction of her love filled his mind, and all else was forgotten.

He hurried home and wrote long and fully to his mother. He told her that his promise to her had been kept, and how much it had cost him to keep it; he tried to describe Margaret, and found his words cold and formal, and he entreated his mother to telegraph and to write without delay. He lay back exhausted after this, and lost himself in the happiest day-dreams.

Soon, soon, the answer would be there, and he could go to her and tell her something of his love for her; something, but not all. It would take a lifetime, he thought, to prove his devotion to her. As he sat thinking happily about it all he did not hear the deep stifled sobs of the poor child upstairs, struggling through anguish and misery. He never dreamed for one moment that he had been misunderstood, and that in trying to say something, in trying to explain without departing from his promise, he had conveyed so false an impression to her.

That parting in the grey light of a rainy day was their real parting—for long—and then all was changed.

When Margaret went down stairs and met her sister and Mr. Sandford she saw that a sudden decision had been come to, and that they were to go, go back to the smoky place they so disliked.

But the great blow that had fallen upon her heart made all else sink to littleness. She was stunned, and no change in their lives, no outside accidents, seemed capable of affecting her.

Next day Sir Albert suffered from the exertion and agitation of the previous one, and was feverish and unwell. The doctor was summoned by his faithful servant, and pronounced him too unwell to rise or to see any one. Not all the prayers of his patient moved him, and then, resigning himself to the inevitable, the young man consoled himself. Had he been able to see Margaret, what had he to say to her? What dared he say till the expected telegram came to set his speech free?

How long the hours seemed! He kept watching the clock and calculating how soon it was possible to hear. His mother was in Wales, and the telegram station was five miles off. He saw it all in his mind's eye. Saw the slow movements of the post-master and the unkempt Welsh pony, and its rider with the letter-bag. Often the boy, glad of the Castle's hospitality on a wet day, would be told to wait and take back the telegram. The hours flew on and no response arrived. Night came and John was sorely put to it to know what to do—his master was evidently worse, and yet he had been annoyed at the doctor being hurried that morning, and had spoken very sharply. What ailed him that he was so unlike himself, so irritable, so anxious?

All this time a tall grave man was hastening to Lornbay—a man bearing grievous tidings to poor Sir Albert Gerald.

While his telegram was speeding on its way, all the hopes and fears and interests of life had ceased for Lady Gerald. She lay dead; having been startled by the news of her son's terrible accident, her slight hold upon life was not strong enough to sustain a shock so great; and that very afternoon, when his promise to her held him back from speaking to Margaret as he longed to speak, she had died with loving messages upon her lips to him. It was in the morning; John, with a grave face and that air of preparedness for coming evil, came to his master and spoke of evil tidings.

Mercifully, the instant those words are breathed we believe the worst, and are so made ready to bear it. Then his uncle, *her* brother Mr. Wynston, went up to his side and told him all.

The tidings were unexpected and terrible to him; he loved her dearly, and all his life had taught him to expect her to be delicate. He was so accustomed to her being an invalid, that he never thought of her as more fragile than other people. And while he wept for her, regardless for the time of all else, his poor little love had gone—with that weary pain of a blighted love to make her still childish heart miserable—for ever?

CHAPTER II.

RENTON PLACE looked black and dingy after the clear air and great beauty of Lornbay. Mrs. Dorriman, always susceptible to those influences of natural external things, shivered, and was depressed, and showed it by the marked effort at cheerfulness she thought was due to her brother.

Mr. Sandford was in a mood difficult to understand. He travelled but a short way with them, avoiding Margaret in a manner that both the girls noticed, and interpreted differently.

He went into a smoking-carriage, chiefly

because they could not follow him there, and he could be free from their observation. He felt thoroughly uncomfortable. He had carried his point with Mr. Drayton, *conditionally*, and Margaret's face, with its wistful expression, hurt him. Yes; though he put it differently to himself, he had virtually sacrificed her to save his own position; and his word was given, and more, he had reluctantly put it down in writing.

Mr. Drayton, while he covered his deepest plans with a jovial laugh that threw every one off their guard, had told him he must have something in writing—not, of course, to show any one, " but as a satisfaction to myself," he said.

Mr. Sandford fought against this point, in vain.

" I do not believe you are in earnest," Mr. Drayton had said. " I will do nothing for nothing. If you intend to help me as you have promised, why make such a fuss about it ? "

" I can only say I will do all I can."

"Then put that in writing."

And Mr. Drayton, with another laugh, wrote out that he (Mr. Sandford) would not leave a stone unturned, but would manage to induce Margaret to marry Mr. Drayton.

When Mr. Sandford had signed it, a strong misgiving crossed his mind. Mr. Drayton's eyes had that look in them that Margaret had noticed; and he felt that remorse, that shrinking from the consequences of his action, that all men, not wholly bad, feel when they act unworthily.

As he sat in the smoking-carriage alone he was conscious of this pang about Margaret, and he was glad to see a total stranger, evidently not an Englishman, get into the carriage.

Anxious to avoid his own thoughts, he broke silence, taking advantage of a turn on their way that opened up an enchanting scene on either side. Waving his hand towards the window, he said, with that air of proprietorship noticeable in some Scotchmen—

"A fine view, sir, a very fine view."

"For God's sake, sir!" exclaimed his fellow-traveller, with a very strong American accent, "do not talk to me of the view. I have a wife and two daughters in another compartment, and I had to come away from them, I am so dead sick of the way they go on about the view. Why upon arth don't you level it all, and grow grain?"

Mr. Sandford was so taken aback at the man's sentiments that he made no further effort in his direction.

He also felt the depression hanging about the air at Renton; but he had placed himself in a position from which he could not escape. He had a few days before him still; then, before Mr. Drayton appeared, he had to say something, and he had to say it in earnest, to Margaret.

It was strange, he thought, that he hated vexing or wounding her in any way. Had she been like Grace, what would it have mattered? But the soft pleading eyes, that look of quiet self-possession, which was so like *her*. He hated by anticipation the look of horror he had seen formerly in her face when Mr. Drayton was in question. He dreaded the coming passage between them, as he seemed never to have dreaded anything before.

Three days came and went, and the very next day Mr. Drayton was to appear, and expected to find that all had gone well, and not one word had Mr. Sandford found the courage to say. Margaret was unusually quiet, even for her; Grace was in a bitter and discontented mood, and tried her sorely. She could not know the weary aching pain that had never left her sister since that fatal interview on the hills. Margaret, who had plenty of spirit generally, and who could parry any remarks she did not like, was now dull and depressed. She had had her dream, and life was a blank to her henceforward. And yet she could not understand it—surely she was not all wrong. And the expression of those dark eyes was speaking the truth perhaps— he did love her and yet was bound. It was all terrible and black as night, before and all around her.

Grace went downstairs the morning Mr. Sandford had resolved to announce his expected guest to Margaret, in a flighty, wild, odd state. She drove Mrs. Dorriman distracted, turned Jean into ridicule, and ended by provoking Mr. Sandford to such an extent that one of his most terrible fits of temper ensued.

He literally raved at her, he ordered her out of the house, and altogether, when Margaret hurried downstairs, he was quite beside himself; there was no insult he could think of he did not fling at Grace, who for once in her life was fairly terrified.

It was Margaret who took her upstairs, Margaret, who, white to her lips, that terrible sense of impending evil pressing upon her, began putting their things together. Grace looked at her blankly, she had a glimmer of its being her fault, and she broke out into murmurs and abuse of Mr. Sandford. " We cannot stay," she said, and Margaret trembling answered her, " No, we cannot stay."

In silence they went on with their preparations; wondering a little that Mrs. Dorriman did not come near them, not knowing that Mr. Sandford prevented her doing so. He never, for a moment, thought Margaret would be such a fool as to go too, and when Mrs. Dorriman suggested this, he got so violent she was forced to draw back.

The girls were ready, and they went downstairs. Mr. Sandford suffering, as he always did, after his fits of passion, was lying back in his chair in his own room, every nerve in his head throbbing, and his head feeling as if it would burst. He heard the door open, and Margaret, yes Margaret, walked in. She was very white and was trembling. He heard her wish him good-bye, and had no power to stop her. She went out gently, and the two forlorn figures left the house, neither of them knowing where to go, full of but one idea, going away and being free.

They had a little money, and neither of them were anxious about ways and means. To the eyes of youth and inexperience, living seems so easy; they had of their own about forty pounds a year; this they thought was quite sufficient; and they would make money; that also seemed so easy in the sublime self-confidence of their youth. They took the train without clearly knowing which station to go to, and, finding that Glasgow seemed to lead everywhere, they went there in the first instance, and then consulting the book they went to a little village among the hills where they thought they might rest quietly and arrange their future plans.

No scenery in the world varies more than does Scottish scenery under the changing influence of the weather. All its rugged grandeur—so splendid bathed in sunlight—so magnificent when partly veiled by those light fleecy clouds that give a subtle charm to its grand hills, and which sends out that marvellous blue colour by the force of contrast

—becomes, under the sullen splash of a downpour of rain dreary, oppressive, and bleak. The rain fell heavily as the two girls stopped at Torbreck, and they looked around them in dismay.

The little station was apart from the village, in the dim distance some small white houses were dotted about. Stacks of peat rose around, and the wide muir on which Torbreck was built was disfigured by the peat-cuttings, now filled with water, which had the deep black tinge of bog-water.

There was no carriage of any kind, the station being a small one of no importance, and having been made chiefly to bring the herds of Highland cattle within reach of the market-town, and for the convenience of a few Highland proprietors who lived some miles off, and who had obtained the concession by yielding their land to the Railway Company on favourable terms.

Leaving their luggage to be sent for, the two girls walked to the village, utterly unconscious of an angry and amazed face that noted their movements.

That day Mr. Drayton had gone to Glasgow *en route* for Renton Place, and he saw the girls at the station, he heard their discussion about the best step, and resolved to find out what it all meant. He had followed them in another part of the train.

Naturally enough he imagined that they were going because of Mr. Sandford's insistance about him, and he was very angry. The man must have bungled in some way, knowing nothing of girls, of Margaret's real character; it seemed to him that she was one of those very gentle quiet people who could be persuaded easily. Why not? He was not an ugly, or an old fellow, he thought. He had all his life been considered handsome. His bright colour and curly hair, his blue eyes and ready laugh, had won him great applause among his few feminine belongings. He had been flattered by most of them, and though his vanity occasionally received a shock, and he sometimes felt himself at a disadvantage, he generally consoled himself quickly. He was too full of self-appreciation to be long unhappy about any slight check, and we all know that every commonest expression is capable of many interpretations. He was too wise to get out at Torbreck, but he stopped at the next station.

The object of his going to Renton was now at an end, and he sat down to think over the position of affairs quietly. After reflecting upon it all he made up his mind to two things, he must know why the girls had left Renton, and he would not tell Mr. Sandford where they were.

He went back to Glasgow, telegraphed to Renton to Mrs. Dorriman that he had been detained, but was on his way there, and would follow his telegram as soon as he possibly could.

Mr. Sandford, in the meantime, was alternating between fits of remorse and despair.

What had he to say when this man came and claimed that "pound of flesh"?

Misfortunes never come singly. That afternoon the post brought letters to Renton Place proving to the master who had so long ruled as with a rod of iron that his sagacity was at fault, and that he who had been for so long a signal mark for success had been proved unwise and that his speculations had failed. It did not mean ruin or even very heavy loss, but it did mean loss of prestige to some extent, and it came at an inopportune moment. There is a certain state of bodily health when a pin-prick may produce disastrous consequences; there is also a corresponding attitude of mind when reverses come with an overwhelming depression, far, far beyond their actual real weight; and then—with that look of happy success characteristic of Mr. Drayton, he arrived, and Mr. Sandford felt that he hated him.

Is it not hard that a man sometimes suffers because nature, ever impartial in the distribution of her gifts, has pointed his nose upwards instead of downwards. He may be full of sublime thoughts, intellectual capacity, and have a decided inclination for poetry, but we credit him with common aspirations only, because of the fluctuation of his nasal organ from the direct perpendicular.

Mr. Drayton might suffer deeply but he never could look miserable; we associate unhappiness with pallor, depressed muscles round the mouth, and drooping eye-lids, and he had a rosy and somewhat beaming face, very round, wide-opened eyes, inclined to stare, and a large mouth wearing a perpetual expression of satisfaction. When the two men confronted each other, Mr. Sandford, whose brow was ruffled with care, and who looked as though he had not slept, could not utter the conventional welcome, he could not speak. Mrs. Dorriman, seeing something unusual, went to his side in fear, and her little, feeble, spasmodic greeting saved both men from a very awkward silence.

"Well," said Mr. Drayton, pleasantly, "and

how are the young ladies? how is Miss Margaret?"

A deep, red flush mounted into Mr. Sandford's face, he turned hurriedly to his sister.

"Leave us," he said, shortly, and she, trembling, obeyed.

"Drayton," he said, in a tone that betrayed effort and agitation, "I had no opportunity of speaking. I intended to keep my word at any cost to myself, but it has been impossible."

"Really," said Mr. Drayton, scornfully. "Well, let me see Miss Margaret and plead my cause with her; let me tell her —— what I must tell her in order that she may understand."

"You cannot see her; she is not here."

"Not here! What do you mean? What foul trick have you played me?"

"I have played you no trick and you need not bluster and take that tone!" answered Mr. Sandford, angrily, his temper rising.

"I have your promise, in words, over and over again, in writing also; I insist on knowing how it all came about. You must have done your spiriting very ungently, perhaps said something unfavourable of me. I declare to you I cannot trust you."

"I never mentioned your name. Grace sent me nearly mad and I said something to her about leaving the house, then Margaret went with her."

"Is this the truth?"

"It is the truth."

"And her leaving this house had nothing to do with me?"

"Nothing whatever."

Mr. Drayton felt that, so far, all was well, but he would not betray any satisfaction to the man before him.

"Those investments I followed your advice about have brought me a loss," he said, after a pause, watching Mr. Sandford's face keenly.

"A loss?"

"Not in money; but my manager has given up his place, and his going is a serious loss. You are really the cause of his departure. He does not believe in you to the same extent other people do. I am sorry, but is there not a proverb about good fish being still in the sea? He was a good man but a trifle too cautious, yes, much too cautious! Well, as Miss Margaret is not here I shall go back."

Mr. Sandford heard this and was uneasy. He knew quite well that Mr. Drayton had no business capacity, and it came home to him very clearly that now that man's influence was withdrawn other people might find the way to his pocket as easily as he had done, when Margaret was in the background.

"I am sorry," he said curtly, relieved to find that he was to be left alone. Mr. Drayton, now Margaret had gone, did not see the use of staying. He made very short adieus to Mrs. Dorriman, and she noticed that he had kept his cab waiting, and had never had his luggage taken off.

"Brother," she said, softly laying her hand upon his arm, "Mr. Drayton has seen Margaret somewhere, he knows where she is. He knew she was not here."

Mr. Sandford stared at her. She sometimes took him by surprise, this under-valued sister of his, and her idea now struck him with surprise. He thought (now that he had time to arrange his ideas) that Drayton had taken the announcement coolly. At the moment it had been a relief, now it confirmed his sister's words. He suspected that she was right, nevertheless it was a sort of surprise to him. It is difficult when one person has habitually put another into a position of inferiority all their lives, and considered them dull, suddenly to change and to credit them with quickness of apprehension. He gave a sort of grunt, and went back to his den. The most important fact now was the resignation of Mr. Drayton's manager. As far as he himself was personally concerned he was glad. Whatever happened now, those lynx-eyes were not in a position to look at the matter confidentially. Still the other side of the question, abovementioned, did not make it altogether pleasant news, and he set himself to think if there was any way in which he could lay a restraining hand upon Mr. Drayton, or rather on Mr. Drayton's speculative tendencies. In the meantime at Torbreck the girls were not doing very well.

They had arrived in a drenched condition at the very small inn, and had applied for a room and for something to go for their luggage.

But, though they got a room, it was fireless, and the luggage a greater difficulty.

There were horses, but they were all busy; the little place, self-contained and prosperous enough, was not prepared for the advent of strangers.

A fire was kindled, but would not burn, the smoke insisted on searching every corner of the room, and if it went up the chimney it came out in puffs in an unexpected and distracting way altogether; the girls sitting there felt their spirits go down to the very lowest ebb, and shivered.

Nothing could be more cheerless than the place — one black horsehair sofa, two rather narrow arm-chairs, and six other chairs, a table that nearly filled up the room in the middle of it, upon which a dusty-coloured worsted mat reposed, three funeral cards of departed relations framed and glazed upon the chimney-piece, and a convex mirror, which reflected and distorted with strict impartiality everything that was there.

After waiting a long time in their wet things, since they had nothing to put on dry till their luggage came, they got some tea and hoped that its warmth would revive them, but the tea was tepid; an accident not unknown to history when there is nothing to keep it hot, and a peat fire, though cheerful to look at and hot enough, does not offer the convenience of a hot plate.

The bedroom close to the sitting-room was as small as it could well be, and the sisters could barely turn round in it. Grace sat looking straight before her. She was feeling very ill. At all times a little fastidious, the second-rate baker's bread (tasting of sawdust) and the uninviting tea, extinguished all wish to eat. She had the painful satisfaction of knowing that her own want of self-control had brought them to this, and yet, poor child, this was nothing to what the future held in store for her, though she did not know it!

The sisters did not speak, they both felt that it was all best endured in silence; they sat, cold and very wretched, till their luggage arrived, then soon creeping into bed they tried to sleep and to forget their misery.

Soon Margaret slept. Her calmer and less exciteable temperament always gave her this advantage, and she slept soundly.

But Grace was sleepless, the shadows of the night oppressed her; long after her sister's regular breathing told its own story she lay tossing wearily from side to side. The small room seemed to stifle her; to the intense cold and shivering she had suffered from, had succeeded burning heat, her head seemed too heavy to lift from her pillow, and it was very early when Margaret was startled by a sharp cry of distress and anguish, and heard Grace saying:

"I am very ill; Oh! Margaret, wake up and do something for me!"

The morning had barely come, the grey dawn, moisture-laden, grew slowly into perfect day; and poor Margaret with a cloak thrown over her, her long fair hair streaming over her shoulders, her sleepy eyes looking wonderingly round her, went downstairs to do her best.

One bare-footed girl was busy, early though it was, and to her Margaret explained herself.

With evident reluctance she went to call her mistress, who came inclined to be cross at losing an hour's much-needed rest.

But crossness vanished when she saw Margaret, and she went upstairs with her; where poor Grace, with a crimson face and panting heavily, lay tossing from side to side and calling her sister.

"How can you leave me when you see how ill I am? I shall die! I know I shall die."

She was frightened, and crying hysterically.

To her immense surprise, Mrs. Munro gave her a good scolding. The surprise was so great that it quieted her, and when that good woman saw the effect she had produced, she left her, to see and get some remedy and to send for the doctor. Before night she was worse, and both knew now that her illness was no light thing. She was suffering acutely, and her illness was pronounced to be inflammation of the lungs.

Mrs. Munro was glad it was "no a catching thing," and was sorry for them. The women of her class in Scotland may be rough, and have a keen eye to a bargain; but their kindness is often wonderful!

Margaret, whose courage always rose when it was needed, neither gave way or got unduly frightened. But she had all the dread of necessary expense that yet could not be met. Grace, always thoughtless and often unreasonable, wanted and asked for a thousand things difficult to obtain, and of course proportionately expensive. Money melted fast. It was impossible to worry Grace, and the burden fell with all its weight upon poor Margaret.

She took counsel with the landlady, and found that she had acted unwisely in so doing. Mrs. Munro had imagined from their appearance and all else that they had plenty of money. Margaret, in her great inexperience, talked of having none, meaning no money for heavy extra expenses. Mrs. Munro, with a sensible loss of respect in her manner, inquired sharply,

"And how am I to be paid, and me doing all I can?"

"I do not mean that," said poor Margaret; "but we are not rich enough, my sister and I, to be able to buy expensive things."

"People should say what they mean," said Mrs. Munro, slightly consoled, but not altogether easy in her mind.

She took counsel with the doctor; and he,

who knew of their connection with Mr. Sandford, and indeed thought the relationship closer than it really was, reassured her on the subject.

"But how comes it then that these two young ladies are stravaging about the country by themselves and na a maid or a soul with them, and they come of rich folk?" asked Mrs. Munro.

"Young ladies have often independent ideas," said Mr. Burns; "but when I was staying with a friend, not far from Renton, the talk there was about the arrival of these young ladies, indeed, I myself saw them there one day walking in the town."

"Well! well! and so I need not be anxious," said Mrs. Munro, much relieved; "but what with gaseous waters and fruits there will be something big to pay; and dear me, Miss Margaret's a nice young lady, she ought to have some one to help, she's nigh worn out already, and it's like to be a time yet before she can see her sister out of bed."

"Her sister is very seriously ill," said the doctor, with a graver face; "I am afraid she is constitutionally delicate. I wonder what her mother died of."

"Oh! I think that will have been a natural-like death, for Miss Margaret said she died in India, and that's a country that kills many folks," she said, comfortably; "they that live come home yellow, and when they don't turn yellow they die."

"Come, come," said Dr. Burns, "I know many that neither turn yellow nor die, that is merely a prejudice."

"It is no prejudice, doctor. I had an uncle once, and he was like one of they dried things they call mummies and show in museums; and people said if you could see his inside it would be all shrivelled up like an old walnut, and I am sure that never was in our family. It was all India; he was a soldier, poor man, and had gone through a deal."

Dr. Burns had no time to carry on the discussion: he was professionally anxious about Grace, she was still so feverish, and, though the acute pain was lessened, her cough was most distressing, and her weakness very great.

"Have you no one to come and help you?" he asked Margaret one day when he had found her worn out, suffering acutely from headache, and in a very depressed state.

"No one," she answered, in a low voice. "I did propose some one to my sister, but she says if she came she would get much worse."

"It is really thoughtless, and, I may say, selfish of her," he said, earnestly. "If my wife were at home I should send her to help you; let me try and get a nurse for you?"

"Oh, no!" said Margaret, earnestly and very eagerly. "I cannot—we cannot afford the expense. I am doing my best, my sister does not suffer from my want of experience," and she looked up very fearfully.

"I am not thinking of her so much as of you," he said, bluntly. Then he went on, in a matter-of-fact tone—"Your sister is better;

the pain is lessened, but the fever still runs high. I do not think she is so strong as you are. What did your mother die of? do you know? She died when you were a baby in India, Mrs. Munro tells me, probably of some fever, did she not?"

"She died of consumption," said Margaret, who did not for a moment see the connection of ideas. Then it flashed across her, and she said, clasping her hands, and in a perfect agony of feeling—"You do not—you cannot—think Grace so ill. Oh! tell me, tell me;" and, weakened by her long watching and hastily-taken meals, she lost her self-command, and cried pitifully.

"I am sorry to have frightened you," said Dr. Burns, who understood her tears, and who, while full of sympathy, spoke in that calm tone which quelled her excitement better than a show of kindness might have done.

"There is no danger at present, absolutely none; but there is great weakness, and very great delicacy."

"What should we do? What ought she to do?" asked Margaret, struggling for her self-command, ashamed of having so completely lost it.

"When she is able for it, she ought to go to some drier climate," he said, looking at the window, where, every now and again, the rain-drops came with a vicious splash, "and, forgive me Miss Rivers, but you cannot command many comforts here. Why do you not write to Mr. Sandford."

"That we cannot do, least of all for Grace!" poor Margaret said unguardedly.

"Of course, I have no right to interfere, but I cannot help feeling interested in the case, and your sister ought to be moved soon; that room is too small for an invalid; the surroundings are too depressing. To be of full use to her you should be cheerful and well; and, bless me! this is not the place for either of you. I would get out of it as soon as I could—if you will forgive my saying so."

He left the room downstairs, where she went

with him each day, to learn, without Grace's overhearing, all he had to say. Margaret stood like a statue after his departure, looking blankly before her, seeing nothing.

What could she do? What was to become of them? She resolved to make one final appeal to her sister about writing to Mrs. Dorriman. If she would consent to this—if she would allow her to endeavour to make friends with Mr. Sandford, all would be well.

If not . . . Margaret came to herself with a start. A horrible conviction began to pierce through all her anxiety. The end would have to be her marriage with Mr. Drayton.

There was nothing else. These two courses alone were open to her. After all, as *he* was not free, did it matter so much what became of her? In all good women's natures there is a vein of self-sacrifice. Her life, she thought, would not have been in vain if she could save her sister. And she did not in the least comprehend Mr. Drayton's character.

She thought him unrefined, noisy, but probably good-hearted and generous. She thought of Grace so completely as a bit of herself that it never for a moment crossed her mind that any one would think of them apart. The absence of all close ties, save that one, made it all in all to her.

Slowly she went upstairs. She would speak to Grace. She would appeal to her. She knew only too well that if she acted without her consent, if she appealed to Mrs. Dorriman, Grace would work herself into a fever; the consequences might be fatal to her. She could not write and not speak, because she knew that she had grown very dear to the poor woman, who had so little outlet for her affections, and that she would come herself to look after them.

When she went into her sister's room she found her asleep; but it was not the sleep of perfect convalescence. There was still much fever, and as poor Margaret watched her tossings and wretched moanings at intervals, her heart sank, and she feared everything!

CHAPTER III.

Sir Albert Gerald hurried to his Welsh home finding the tediousness of his journey and the inevitable jolting of the railway-carriage almost beyond his strength.

John remonstrated in vain. To the young man there was something tragical in his mother's death, apart from the only being she loved and clung to.

That doubt that visits most people when one loved is gone, as to whether we have in any way failed towards them, visited him now. Even his new passion for Margaret was for the moment pushed upon one side, and he would, he must, be beside her, see her once more; and he would not allow any personal ease or want of strength to stay him.

The result might have been guessed by all. When he got home he carried out his wish, he did see that loved face once more, but a return of the acute internal pain stretched him on his bed, and the local doctor, fearing for him in his reduced state, gave him opiates, and so kept him from consciousness and suffering at the same time.

Afterwards, what pain he would willingly have borne! had he been allowed full consciousness.

It was some weeks before he emerged from the darkened room, and his first act was to find out Margaret's address.

But, though he learned the sisters had gone from Lornbay, no one knew where, and when his pressing letters stirred a friend into action, and that he actually went to Renton, it was only to find that they were no longer there, and that even Mrs. Dorriman had not their address.

To her he wrote and made no secret of his anxiety to find Margaret, but with the best will in the world (and she sincerely liked Sir Albert) she could say nothing, knowing nothing.

At that very time Margaret was trying to resign herself to a fate she dreaded for the sake of Grace.

When on that memorable evening the doctor had spoken out his fears, and Margaret had watched by her sister's bedside, she had noticed the hollow cheeks and listened to her distracting cough, she absolutely hated herself for shrinking from any sacrifice and so save her.

Had she had one shred of hope in connection with Sir Albert it would have been impossible, but she had no hope; and more than this, the terrible stab to her pride, the feeling that she had given her love without its being really sought, maddened her at times. He would hear of her, if she married Mr. Drayton, and he would never know the truth.

Grace woke in a paroxysm of pain and terror; till now she had suffered acutely, but there had been no hæmorrhage, now it came on, and poor Margaret, terrified and dreading she knew not what, was driven to despair. Standing by her sister and watching her agonized face she took a solemn vow that at any cost to herself she would save her.

After a night of bitterest anguish and suffering came peace, and Margaret slept on the hard little sofa, slept profoundly through all the stir and bustle of the " Sun " till the afternoon.

There was a shaded light in the room, and when she woke it was with the consciousness of some one gazing at her, which most of us have known by experience. Startled and confused, her lovely eyes still heavy with sleep, and her hair in disorder, she sat up and looked round her.

There, sitting like a silent fate, on the opposite side of the room, was the man she dreaded, Mr. Drayton, who was intently watching her.

Margaret started to her feet, a burning blush rising to her face.

"How did you come here?" she said. "Why did Mrs. Munro let you come upstairs?"

"I have been at Renton, Margaret" (she never noticed that he spoke her name familiarly) "Do you think I could stop away when I knew that you were wandering and by yourself?"

"My sister has been very ill, she is very ill," poor Margaret said, trembling.

"A bad place to be ill in," he said. "No comforts, let alone luxuries. "Now what can I do for you? make a friend of me. I will do what I can, and I will do it willingly for *your* sake."

Margaret could not speak. She had thought everything possible a few hours before, and now ——- Why did that sound of the sea fill her ears, that sound that made a grand chant as an accompaniment to other words and other tones? She pressed back that memory. Mr. Drayton was again speaking.

"I trust you will let me be of use," he was saying, wondering what caused that flush of consciousness that came into her face and died away again.

"You are very good," she said, in a low voice.

He made one or two steps nearer her, and, in that small room this brought him close. She shrank back involuntarily, and he saw the movement and it made him savage. But he controlled himself; he began to understand a little of her character; if he intended to win he must be cautious.

"I will go now," he said, taking her cold little hand in his, "but I will not go far, and you *must* think of me as your friend; will you?"

Again came the faintly-uttered words,

"You are very good."

He gave one lingering look at her and went

downstairs, calling Mrs. Munro in a sharp, quick tone.

"Mr. Sandford requested me to see that the sick young lady and her sister had every comfort you can provide. Can you think of anything?"

"Oh dear, sir!" said poor Mrs. Munro, immensely relieved by this declaration, "that poor thing ought to have a nurse, and I've said so over and over again but Miss Margaret she seems afraid of spending. I was quite sure, sir, myself, it would be all right, such young ladies as these are, poor things; and Miss Margaret would not buy herself a sofa—a sofa to sleep on—and I have done my best, having my own work and the house on my hands, and responsibility; night work is not in my way, sir; but the scores of times I've been up and down those stairs, they're not much to look at but they're tiresome to go up and bad to come down when it comes to being often, sir."

"Buy what is wanted and let me know what it is, for Mr. Sandford. Anything wanted you are to get at once, and you need not worry Miss Margaret or say I have had a hand in it. She might not like my meddling. I am Mr. Sandford's acquaintance more than hers and I am acting for him." He went out of the house without waiting to hear her answer.

Then he went to the doctor's house and cross-questioned him. He learned from him what was wanted, and played his part well. Dr. Burns was delighted that Mr. Sandford was now taking up their case, and telegraphed for a nurse and various things he thought necessary without loss of time.

Margaret's surprise was unbounded; she never for one moment doubted the truth of the landlady's story, and was too completely worn out to question the nurse closely when she came. She knew Mr. Sandford was really generous, and she thought that, having heard of Grace's illness from Mr. Drayton, he was trying to help her, and she expected to see Mrs. Dorriman's pleasant face appear at any moment.

The choicest fruit, the rarest flowers, everything money could procure, arrived without stint, and Grace began to revive. Margaret took the first opportunity of writing a long letter to Mrs. Dorriman; her heart overflowed, she thanked her for all her thoughtfulness and kindness, said how often she had wished herself with her sympathetic kindness to help her, and sent a message full of kindly feeling to Mr. Sandford. She had just completed her letter, written with difficulty, since Grace claimed her every moment and the interruptions, added to the trouble she had of showing her gratitude and expressing her sorrow without reflecting on her sister's short-comings, when Mr. Drayton came in.

"You have been writing," he said, seeing what her occupation had been.

"Yes, I have been thanking dear Mrs. Dorriman for being so thoughtful and so kind about my sister. All the luxuries, the better nursing, so many comforts, are saving her life," and Margaret's eyes were softer than ever, and moist with feeling. "I can never thank her enough."

"Is there so much to be grateful for?" he asked, in a tone she could not quite understand, and did not, at the moment, pause to consider.

"Ah, you cannot know what it was before," she said, fervently; "to see my poor sister dying and not to know how to help her, and then to see her reviving; and you have been kind, too," she added, as a faint colour came into her cheek, "and I believe you told Mrs. Dorriman. Indirectly we owe it to you, and I am grateful to you."

He was thrown off his guard.

"Margaret," he said, hoarsely, "would it pain you to owe it *all* to me? If your letter is to thank Mrs. Dorriman then do not send it for I never wrote to her. Those things and the attendance you think so much of, trifles in themselves, are really for you from me. I would die to serve you! These seem but little things."

Margaret, startled and alarmed, looked at him with dismay and even terror in her face; she felt as though the meshes of a net were being drawn together and that she was being suddenly made to feel all efforts at escape were powerless.

Mr. Drayton still watched her keenly. Would this avowal help him or keep her further from him?

"How can I thank you?" she said at last, with white and trembling lips.

"You know how. Do not speak, for if you spoke just now you might destroy all my hopes of happiness. I know," he said, bitterly, "that not only you do not love me but that you positively shrink from being under any obligation to me. But, Margaret, think it over. I am ready to do all I can, and you have no one else. I would be content to love you; I do not expect that a young and beautiful girl like you can return my passion."

He stopped short. Margaret sat silent, cold as a very statue.

"Think it over," he repeated, and his voice was full of pathos and passion. "And, when you have decided, send me one word, *come*. Till then I will leave you in peace."

He rose and left her, and the poor child sat on with the dazed feeling of helplessness that sometimes follows the news of some great calamity, hardly able to think, her head in a perfect whirl.

She was roused by the nurse, who told her her sister wanted her.

Then one ray of hope came to her; she would speak of it to Grace; she thought, now Grace was better and more capable of forming an opinion, she would herself wish to prevent this way of escape and that she would think of going back and propose it. She went to her, into the larger room Mr. Drayton had insisted upon her having, and went up to the sofa where Grace lay placid, surrounded by flowers and things *he* had sent her.

"Grace," she said, kneeling by her and looking in her sister's face with a world of protest and anxiety in her eyes, "when you are quite well again you would not mind giving up luxuries. When you are really yourself again you will not fear poverty?"

"Margaret, what do you mean?" exclaimed Grace, in agitated tones; "these things, as you call them, are necessities to me now."

"But, if to have them, Grace, I was forced to do something I very much hate doing, that would spoil my life for always; you would do without things when you are well, Grace? And we might go back."

"You may do what you like, Margaret, just as you choose, but I never will go back to that odious man and that detestable place."

"Not if it saved me from life-long sorrow?"

"That is nonsense, Margaret. I know quite well what you mean; you mean that you do not want to marry Mr. Drayton, and you have all kinds of high-flown ideas; why, if you married him we should be happy always, and I do hate poverty!" and Grace feebly drew her quilt—one of his gifts—up to her ears.

"But, Grace," pleaded Margaret, craving for one little word of comfort or help, "I have such a strong conviction that such a marriage is a wicked thing to do. I think it is so wrong to marry when love is not there. It is such a solemn thing, Grace. It is like doing wrong deliberately."

"You make everything solemn," said Grace, in a peevish tone; "I am asking you to do nothing I would not do myself. If Mr. Drayton asked me to marry him I would say 'yes,' directly."

"But we are different."

"Yes, we are different; and now you have made me miserable. I shall do nothing now but lie still and expect to see all my comforts vanish," and a violent fit of coughing silenced her.

That afternoon she was worse; the excitement of the conversation had been too much for her. When night came on once again the terrible hæmorrhage came on. Even the nurse upbraided Margaret.

"Your sister was doing so well till you went to talk to her," she said; "young people never can be made to understand how very quiet a person in Miss Rivers's state should be kept. Another attack like this might be fatal to her."

All night Margaret watched and prayed alternately. Her spirits were in a feverish, excited state. She was wild with remorse one moment and in despair the next. The attack was dreadful to witness in itself, and Grace's deep terror made it all the more terrible.

When morning dawned a note lay on the table addressed to Mr. Drayton. It was an appeal that might have moved any one not selfishly bent on his own end. Margaret asked him if he thought a marriage could be happy for either of them where upon her side lay no love. "I am grateful to you, but gratitude is different if you insist upon this proof. You are making me do wrong, no blessing will follow." She wrote this hoping, trusting to his generosity. But as she sent it she said to herself it was her last chance—that if her words did not move him now her sacrifice would have to be complete. Grace lay prostrate, too languid to take notice of anything, too much exhausted to be able to speak.

The doctor was distressed, and poor Margaret felt an indirect reproach was conveyed to her in the urgent words to the nurse about "Keep Miss Rivers quiet; agitation, the least excitement, will prove fatal."

"And this step, by which alone it seems I can save her, kills my life also," Margaret breathed softly to herself.

Mr. Drayton did not, in the least, understand all the poor child meant to convey in her letter; the one fact made all others of no account—Margaret would marry him, and he had gained his point.

Mr. Sandford would have seen something in his face, had he been there, which Margaret had seen long ago. His steel-blue eyes gleamed with triumph and a curious shifting light.

He went to the "Sun," as soon as he possibly could, and Margaret read her fate in his expression; and her heart seemed to die within her.

* * * * *

Some weeks passed away. Where had Margaret learned all the caution she showed now? She was going to make a sacrifice. The instinct of self-preservation made her write to Mr. Sandford; she insisted upon seeing him at once, and Mrs. Dorriman she entreated to come to her.

Mr. Drayton was very much annoyed when he found what she had done. "They will take you away," he said; "they will come between us."

"I have given you my promise," she said, coldly, "is not that enough?"

There was no room in the little inn for either, but Margaret took some lodgings. It was the best, as their presence would have agitated Grace too much.

Mr. Sandford found a new Margaret in the cold, calm resolute girl before him.

She told him shortly and very quietly that she had promised to marry Mr. Drayton.

"But I no longer wish it," he said eagerly, and hoping to see her soften and change. Her hard, cold expression was a terrible disappointment.

"I have promised," she answered, "and I wanted you to come because, if I do this, it is for Grace; and you must manage for me, that, if I live or die, Grace will be cared for. She must have plenty, always. You are wise about things, and clever. I give my life, and Grace must have plenty."

"But, Margaret! Is Grace worth this? A tiresome, wrong-headed, selfish creature ——"

"Please spare her to me!" said Margaret, passionately; "she is my sister, and I love her."

"But surely ——"

"I have promised," repeated Margaret, and Mr. Sandford controlled his temper. He said, quietly,

"Only say one thing, that I am not the cause ——"

"I cannot say it," said Margaret, vehemently; "you offered us a home, and you made that home unbearable."

"You are ungenerous."

"Were you generous when you taunted us, when you said we were to go?"

"I never said so to you."

"You said it to Grace, my sister, whom I love better than my life."

Then his temper rose, and he said cruel and bitter things of Grace; and Margaret stood up, and, resuming her reserve and coldness, faced him.

"It is nothing to you," she began, in low tones, "you say these things, and expect me to hear them. I do not value your love for me—if you do love me as you say—because you will extend no forbearance to my sister.

You cannot separate us—in feeling. She is part of myself, and—for her sake—things can be met that would otherwise be impossible."

Mr. Sandford was silent. He never realised the effect of his violence, and he was conscious of so much liking for Margaret that he thought her ungrateful for not returning his affection in some degree.

"I will have neither act nor part in this marriage," he said, rising.

"You will not help me, so far, then?" she asked, wearily, "and I have no one else."

Mr. Sandford wrote an address down.

"This man will help you," he said, hiding his uncomfortable feelings under an increase of gruffness. "He is a lawyer, and will arrange matters. As for me, I am of no use, and I wash my hands of all your concerns henceforward."

He left her feeling more forlorn than before. She was conscious now of having had a vague hope, in some way, of his arranging things for her and Grace, of having received kindness.

She felt that loyalty to her sister demanded that she should resent his words; and she resolutely pushed away any regrets from her.

Then she sat down, and began to write to the address given to her. She found it difficult to write, most difficult to express herself; and as she sat thinking how best she could give—that most dangerous thing—a half-confidence, the door was pushed open gently, and Mrs. Dorriman, her face working with suppressed agitation, entered and took her in her arms.

Mrs. Dorriman had gone to Torbreck thinking that she had some news to give which would change matters very much for Margaret, and, therefore, not so overwhelmed by the news of her engagement to Mr. Drayton as she would otherwise have been.

After tearful inquiries about Grace, and many gentle exclamations of sorrow and wonder, she thought she would say something to Margaret about Mr. Drayton; she would be cautious. She was too timid to act upon her own conviction, she would be guided by her answer.

"Are you really engaged to Mr. Drayton, my dear Margaret, quite engaged to him?"

"I have promised," said poor Margaret.

"But, perhaps, my dear, I could tell you something."

"You must tell me nothing," she exclaimed, quickly. "I have promised—and—you must not make it harder for me."

"Then it is hard?"

"I am giving up my life!"

"But perhaps, Margaret, what I have to say may change ——."

"Nothing can change things now," and Margaret spoke firmly; "I cannot go back, and he has done so much."

"It is such a miserable mistake," and poor Mrs. Dorriman thought how she could say a word, "others would do as much ——."

"But Grace will not have it. No! do you think I should have consented, do you think I would consent, if it had been possible. . . . . .

Oh!" she exclaimed and a look of terror came into her eyes, "even this is wrong. I should not speak of it so. Dear!" she continued, turning to poor bewildered Mrs. Dorriman, "you must help me, and not let me feel that you do not understand me. I have thought about it and prayed about it, and I must go through with it." She paused to regain her self-command, and then added, " and there is no one else."

"There is no one else," repeated Mrs. Dorriman, vaguely; "I thought there was somebody else."

Had she too seen that dawning passion which Margaret had stifled so vehemently? A burning flush rose to her face, and she answered angrily, "There is no one else."

And then they talked of other things.

After this Mrs. Dorriman held her peace. She wisely felt that in telling Margaret of Sir Albert's visit, and dwelling, as she intended to have dwelt upon, his anxiety to find her—she might be doing no good, and only making mischief.

Mr. Drew, the lawyer to whom Margaret wrote, was accustomed to the vaguest statements possible, made him, from time to time, by his feminine clients. But he thought that in the whole course of his experience he had never read anything so impossible to understand as poor Margaret's effusion.

He could only make out two facts. She wanted a good deal of money made safe in some way (as she had none herself), she was going to be married; then she contradicted this and said *she* wanted no money. It was only her sister.

As she named Mr. Sandford, and Mr. Drew had a slight business acquaintance with him, he wrote to him, and received enlightenment.

"Miss Margaret Rivers has made up her mind to marry a man for his money, and wishes to make sure that his part of the bargain is put beyond business losses; the money is wanted for her sister, Miss Grace

Rivers, and you had better take good care what you are about, as Mr. Drayton, the man in question, is as slippery as an eel."

Luckily poor Margaret knew nothing of this explanation. Mr. Drew came to Torbreck to see her. He expected to find an elderly shrewd woman, and he was more surprised than he could say, when he was suddenly confronted with Margaret.

His astonishment was so great that he stood before her speechless for a little while.

"Miss Margaret Rivers?" he said, inquiringly.

"Yes, Margaret Rivers is my name. I wrote to you. I am sorry you have had to take the trouble of coming."

"Your letter was a little difficult to understand," he said, smiling, and no longer wondering at its vague nature. How could this young girl enter into explanations with a stranger? and he was so amazed to think she was going to marry Mr. Drayton he could not get over it. What was the motive?

But Margaret, having got over the hardest part of all, her own consent, in a grave, matter-of-fact way, tried to say what she had to say plainly.

"Mr. Drayton has promised —— my sister must be safe ——" this was all she had to say.

"And you yourself, Miss Rivers?"

"I want nothing, nothing for myself, but for her—it must be made safe."

"I do not see how that can be done unless *she* marries Mr. Drayton. Any money arrangement must take the form of a marriage settlement."

She looked at him blankly.

"Is this so? is this quite true?"

"It is quite true. There may be a stipulation, a promise, but, forgive me, Miss Rivers, that would look like a bargain and might lead to misconception."

"It is a bargain," said poor Margaret, while her face crimsoned under his gaze; "my sister, in some way, must be made secure."

"I think I had better see Mr. Drayton's

man of business," he said, finding that she cared for nothing but what could be done for her sister.

"A clear case of being bought and sold," he said to himself as he left her; "what a pretty, attractive girl! Well, I shall take care to look sharply after her interests."

It was, however, very difficult indeed to get Mr. Drayton to come to any arrangement. He was entirely taken by surprise. Had Mr. Sandford done this of course it would have been only right and what might have been expected; but Margaret, to give instructions to a lawyer and to stipulate about money matters! He went to her, angry and annoyed.

"You might trust me," he said.

"How can I trust life?" she said, with a solemn, grave look; "death is always there, and if you died——my sister might suffer. I may die . . . . . It must be so."

He shivered a little.

"How you go on, talking of death, Margaret; and you never smile; you are not like any bride I ever saw, you look so mournful, so sad; do you know you are paying a very bad compliment? Will it satisfy you if I arrange for that precious sister of yours to have something at my death?"

"No," said Margaret, firmly, "you know that I am only marrying you because I cannot help myself and her. I have never hidden the truth from you, never; if you insist on marrying me I have concealed nothing from you... It is not yet too late."

He looked steadily at her.

"I cannot imagine why I love you so much," he said, bitterly, "in spite of your scorn, your coldness, and all else. I think I am indeed a fool."

"Why do you care so much?" she said; "there are many who might learn to love you, many girls fairer than I am. I am not so very fair."

"There is but one Margaret for me," he answered, "and in time you will love me," and yet he had an uneasy sense of inferiority, of not being able to reach her standard.

Mr. Drew found him a very troublesome and a very difficult man to deal with, and after all he could not make the arrangement he wished. Margaret would be hemmed in with restrictions, and trustees would have much in their power; a very modest sum was secured to Grace in the event of Mr. Drayton's death. In short, it came to this; that both sisters were dependent upon him during his life, and were provided for, Margaret very amply, at his death.

Mr. Drew's objections were overruled by Margaret.

"All I wanted was a certainty in the event of being left alone. Of course, while I live, while *we* live, Grace will share everything with me. Mr. Drayton will allow this."

He said nothing, imagining that he had promised this. In her inexperience she never dreamed of a life apart from Grace. Of course she would be with her; they would share everything; that was so completely in her mind that the poor child never dwelt upon it, she took it for granted. She received various letters from old school-fellows when her approaching marriage was made known, but she could not answer them. She laid them aside, and would write afterwards. How could she answer congratulations? One letter from a girl she had liked particularly, remained before her for a long time.

"I am longing to know all about *him*," she wrote. "After the intimacy between us I have felt your silence hard; it is now explained; you are happy in having found your ideal already; I was always afraid that few could come up to your high standard, and you are not the sort of character to marry without both love and esteem."

Poor Margaret! Already her quick-sightedness, unblinded by love, showed her Mr. Drayton as he was— vain, and led by his vanity alone. He was good-humoured in all else and inclined to be kind, but if he was not upon good terms with himself, if he was not flattered, his good-humour vanished and he became rude and sulky. And Margaret, among other things, dreaded his rudeness, and, but for that prostrate figure so indescribably dear to her, would have died rather than have faced life with him. To her it was a moral death, and not the least painful part of the sacrifice was, that, while she could see nothing else, she fell in her own esteem.

It was a forlorn little ceremony altogether. Mrs. Dorriman, who clung faithfully to the poor child, went with her to Glasgow, where Mr. Drayton had made all the necessary arrangements.

Nothing less like a bride ever went to the altar. All the time the ceremony went on Margaret heard nothing, thought of nothing, but was uttering fervent prayers for forgiveness and help. There was a hurried farewell. Mrs. Dorriman saw them into the train—they were going away for a little time.

As she still stood there Margaret turned her

tearful eyes towards the man who was now her husband.

"When shall we return? I want to send a message to my sister."

For all answer he repeated to her the words she had just uttered,

"'Forsaking all others, cleaving only to him,'" and, as he spoke, the train started.

CHAPTER IV.

Grace lay back after parting from Margaret with a sense of having at length got her foot upon sure ground; but there was not that entire sense of satisfaction which she had expected. The remembrance of Margaret's white face and the quivering lips was not pleasant. It was quite Margaret's way to take high ground about everything—she saw everything in an exaggerated way; that came of having such a poetical temperament, which was not always a desirable thing.

In spite of these sensible reflections there was a strong sense of discomfort, and, though Grace tried to shake it off and read and talk to the nurse, that did not help her. The nurse dwelt upon the beautiful bride her sister would be; never for a moment doubting orange-blossom, white satin, and all complete.

Mrs. Dorriman came home late and went into Grace's room with signs of tears, due partly to the sadness of that wedding and partly to fatigue. Grace's light questions jarred upon her. She felt that it had been a terrible sacrifice, and she wished that the sister who understood it so little could be made to appreciate it. "Poor darling Margaret!" said Grace, "did she send me no message?"

"She had no time. I heard her ask him when they should be home—she wished to let you know. I heard his answer. *Forsaking all others, cleaving only to him.* My mind misgives me, Grace; that poor child will not have all she hopes and expects from him."

"You must not be so doleful, Mrs. Dorriman, it is so very bad for me," said Grace, peevishly.

"I am sorry," said that poor woman, who did not wish to hurt her. "I was not thinking of you, I was thinking of Margaret."

"Every one is always thinking of Margaret," went on Grace, in a fretful tone. "It is the most extraordinary thing, it is always the same thing—it is always Margaret."

"Rest now, and we can talk by-and-by," said Mrs. Dorriman. "I have much to do; and about you, Grace, have you any plans?"

"Have I any plans?" asked Grace, opening her eyes in deepest astonishment. "Why, as soon as I can move, of course, I am to go to live with Margaret—a lovely villa with trees and things, close to London!"

"Oh, then that is settled," said Mrs. Dorriman, very much relieved. "I did not know; it will be nice for you to be together."

"Yes, it will be nice, said Grace, excitedly. "If you knew how I long to go away and see the world."

"Poor child!"

"Now, Mrs. Dorriman, there you are as

doleful as you can be again. I wish you would not —— "

" Would not do what ? "

" Speak as if I were never to be well again," and Grace, feeble and weak, burst into a violent flood of tears.

" I was not thinking of *that*," said Mrs. Dorriman, hastily, " but life is disappointing, and if you cling to the world too much you will feel the many disappointments overwhelmingly."

" Wait till you see," said Grace, hastily brushing her tears away.

Mrs. Dorriman left her; she had not the courage to tell her her own conviction that Mr. Drayton might be kind to her in the matter of money, but as to her living with him and with Margaret, making it in short her home, *that* she thought entirely unlike him to propose. However, she knew nothing really about the matter. What had passed between the sisters, or what arrangements and stipulations she had made with Mr. Drayton, were equally out of her knowledge, and she trusted from Grace's confident manner that she had something tangible to go upon.

In the meantime Mr. Sandford urged his sister's return, and the doctor was anxious to get Grace to a more congenial climate.

She had certainly been better and brighter lately, and he hoped, if she went somewhere in time, she might yet get well.

Mrs. Munro was extremely offended by his way of disparaging the climate. "What ails you that you are for aye backbiting our climate. If water goes up it's bound to come down somewhere."

"But it is all coming down here just now," he said, laughing, "and it is very damp. It is all very well for you and me, Mrs. Munro, we are both strong and healthy, but that poor young lady will never get well unless we can get her away."

"I don't know about damp," she said. "With a good house over one's head (and this is a good house), and fires, what does the weather outside matter? It's just fidgets, doctor, and nothing else."

The good doctor could not quite understand the hitch. Mrs. Dorriman had written to her brother. She was surprised at Grace's quiescence; forgetting that in the extreme languor of early convalescence we accept things without question, and the fatigue of puzzling over the future is often spared us.

Mr. Sandford was not at all stingy, but he had liked Margaret and had wished to be kind to her, and he blamed Grace for having upset all his arrangements, and most of all for this marriage.

Several things had happened lately which made him think of Mr. Drayton in a very different light; and he was angry with Margaret for having married him, and angry with himself for having once wished her to do so.

His temper did not improve with age. He was more irritable than ever. He found fault with everything, and had Jean been writing to Mrs. Dorriman she might have added with truth the word " rampageous " now.

Mrs. Dorriman appealed to him for money to take Grace south. "She is ill and you are not, and in her state of health I feel it would be cruel to send her away alone."

Her letter reached him at a wrong moment. He had just had what he considered a most impertinent letter from Mr. Drayton, and he sat down, and in the roughest language told his sister plainly that the Draytons might look after Grace, he would never have anything more to do with her; and he insisted upon *her* returning to him immediately.

Poor Mrs. Dorriman! She went to see Grace not knowing how she was to announce her departure, imagining that the girl would feel so forlorn without her sister or herself; perplexed as to how the doctor's wishes were to be carried out, and altogether worried and annoyed.

Grace was in very high spirits. "See, Mrs. Dorriman," she called out, gaily, "I can walk quite firmly across the room!" and with a very faltering step she tottered against the opposite wall.

Her attenuated figure and glistening eyes filled Mrs. Dorriman with compassion, and it was with a great effort she said, when Grace, panting a little, was once more on her sofa, "When did you hear from Margaret last, my dear?"

"A week ago; she is so lazy about writing, and when she writes she tells me nothing," said Grace, very pettishly.

"Where did she write from?"

"Some place in Austria—just imagine what luck for her going to Vienna, Paris, Berlin, and Constantinople."

"Did she give you any address?"

"Oh, she never does, because she never has the least idea where she is going to. Mr. Drayton keeps it all to himself, I fancy. I have written to her, but I send my letters on chance. Stay, I think I have her last letter here, you may see it if you like. Poor Margaret, she always takes life so very seriously, she has no sense of fun. I am sure with her opportunities I should have written a much longer and a more amusing letter!"

Mrs. Dorriman read the letter, and her eyes filled with tears. It was a letter written by one who has lost all the spring of youth—unhappiness was on its every page, and the craving to know that Grace was well and surrounded with comforts, and that she was happy. It was a beseeching cry to know if the step she had taken had been of use to her beloved sister.

"Grace," said Mrs. Dorriman, after a moment or two, "when you move, as the doctor hopes, have you money?"

"Money! My dear Mrs. Dorriman, what an odd question. I have no money—A few shillings, that is all."

"And will Margaret send you some? Will Mr. Drayton pay all your expenses?"

"Of course he will, now Margaret has married him. I see what you mean. I had better write to her about it."

"Yes, you had better write." Mrs. Dorriman's face flushed. "I wish, my poor child, it had been otherwise, but my brother is still offended with you. I am so very sorry, but he wants me to go home to him."

"Does he?" said Grace, indifferently, and Mrs. Dorriman noticed with a pang that this news she had thought necessary to break to the invalid did not affect her at all.

"He wants me at once. I do not like leaving you alone here, Grace, without your sister; it will be dull for you and lonely."

"It would be, but you see I am going too," said Grace. "If I do not hear from Margaret soon I shall go to London to their house and wait for them there."

She spoke so confidently that Mrs. Dorriman was much relieved. With all her compassion there was so little that was congenial to her that she never could be affectionate to Grace, and she herself being of a warm-hearted nature fancied that the girl must miss it in her. She was always trying to like her, and failing.

The letter Grace wrote at intervals, and with some difficulty, reached Margaret after some delay. She was on the Rhine at Mayence, tired out with incessant travelling, and most anxious about her sister. She waited impatiently for her husband's return, he had gone out on business.

"I have heard from Grace, written after she had walked across the floor by herself. She is able to travel now. When can we get home?" she asked, as he entered the little sitting-room.

He laughed a little. "So Miss Grace is able to travel. Where does she intend going to?" he asked blandly.

Margaret's face flushed. "She is coming to us—she is to live with us."

"This is indeed news," he said, laughing—and how she had grown to hate his laugh! "There are two sides to that statement."

"You cannot surely object to my sister coming to pay me a visit."

"I am afraid I do object—between such a devoted couple as you and I," he said, with a sneer. "No third person would find it pleasant. I do not intend trying it, at any rate."

"You do not mean to say that my own and only sister may not come to me?" said Margaret, her voice faltering.

"I do mean it. I married you; I did not marry your sister also. She is not quite in my line, and the sooner you understand it the better."

"And poor child, she is ill, and ... penniless." Margaret's heart beat to suffocation. She had married for this one thing, and had not got what she had considered a certainty.

"It is cruel to keep us apart," she said, choking back her tears, feeling helpless and miserable.

"It is a sad position," he said, with his hateful little laugh. "But perhaps excellent Mr. Sandford will provide for her."

"And you know," said Margaret, indignantly, "you know that our being at Torbreck was because Grace could not bear the position he put her in. She cannot bear him!"

"How unfortunate! Well, you see, I do not like her at all. Why should I? She has never shown me decent civility, and I do not choose to have her. It is better to be frank with you. I hate all her d——d airs and graces."

Margaret's tears were falling fast. Stifling her emotion she summoned up her courage. She said, "I have never asked you for money, will you give me some now?"

"To send to her—certainly not."

"You will not give any money," she exclaimed, in despair.

"No, I will do nothing of the kind. Now, Margaret, you had better understand me once for all. When I married you I intended to win your love. I did not expect you ever to give me what I gave you. You have never once given me a spontaneous mark of affection. You look as though you were brokenhearted, and a martyr. Do you suppose that I did not know that you only married me because that precious sister of yours had chosen to quarrel with her bread and butter? But I did not care. I thought kindness and affection would win something in return. I consider that, as you fail in your side of the bargain, I have every right to fail in mine." And with one of his detestable laughs he left her to think over his words.

Margaret went to the open window and looked on the garden and the river—brilliant in the sunshine and seeming to mock at her despair.

There was that painful grain of truth in his words that filled her with humiliation. Was she not justly punished? She had done wrong; could good ever come out of evil? She might live long, and all her life she was to have this terrible companionship.

She clasped her hands together, and tried to think calmly and prayerfully what she could do now, when the silence of humanity amidst the throb and ripple of the river was broken, and a well-remembered voice was calling her by name.

"Margaret, my Margaret, I have found you! I am free to tell you the end of my story. I tried to tell you the beginning. I love you! My darling, I love you! Can you love me in return!"

A faint cry burst from Margaret's lips. For a few moments the present and all the horrors of her position fell away from her memory. He stood beside her, and, reading nothing but the flood of joy with which she heard his words in her face, he clasped her in his arms.

For one delicious moment Heaven seemed to open to her. She forgot everything but that he loved her. Then with a cry she pushed him away from her, and stood hiding her face in her hands, too wretched, too utterly miserable, for tears or any outward expression. He stood aghast; he had seen the joy in her face and now what did this mean?

She turned towards him hurriedly; he must not stand there; he must not be left for one moment in ignorance. With suppressed passion she told him all, how she had misinterpreted his words, and how she had tried to forget him; of her sister's illness, and of her own marriage. Once she began to speak the words rushed from her lips. She told him of her cruel and bitter disappointment about Grace, and she asked him wildly to help her. "What am I to do!" she cried. "Help me!"

He heard her with the bitterest feeling against the man who had used her love for her sister, only in the end to break faith with her. It was terrible to him to see Margaret, always so calm and so self-possessed, in such deep and terrible agitation. His grief for her was so powerful that his own sank into nothingness beside it. He had always thought her great unselfishness one of her greatest perfections, but the devotion to her sister was to him quite wonderful.

In calm tones that did not yet entirely hide the agitation he fain would conceal from her, he, upon his side, explained his promise to his mother, and his journey and her death. Through all her misery came the clearing away of a cloud. She had not erred, and he had loved her!

They stood side by side, silent after that lifting of the veil from both their hearts, he noting with agony the transparency which filled him with alarm.

She had asked him for help, and he would help her.

"Let me have your sister's address," he said; "there is only one thing I want now to understand, why did Mrs. Dorriman never tell you of my visit?"

"Mrs. Dorriman?"

"Yes! Finding I could get no news of you I went there and saw her. She did not know where you were, but I let her see how anxious I was to find you. I let her know I loved you, Margaret; did she never speak of me to you?"

"Never," said poor Margaret, falteringly. "Ah!" she said, as a sudden gleam came to her memory, "I remember now she tried to tell me something, and I would not listen. I did not know—how could I know—it referred to you?"

"Would it have been too late?" he asked, in a low voice.

"I do not know," she said, passing her hand across her tearless eyes. "I cannot say what I might have done; but then I had promised —— Is it not hard?" she exclaimed. "Oh! it does seem hard, to have had happiness within my grasp and to have lost it!"

He was inexpressibly affected, afraid of making things harder for her; he moved to go.

"You will always be to me my highest type of womanhood," he said. "Will you trust me about your sister? I will go to England to-night."

"Let us say farewell now and for ever," she said, stretching out her hands, and then as he wrung them in his she breathed "God bless you," and so passed out of his sight.

Sir Albert lost no time; he knew it was

best, and he made all his arrangements, and left by the first train he could catch.

His one comfort now would be doing something for her through her sister. But when the bustle of the departure was over and he was ensconced in his railway-carriage he had time to think of his own most cruel and terrible trial. Ever since he had begun to know Margaret his love for her increased. He had wandered to regain health and strength. Her image was never out of his mind, and he had believed he had made things so clear to her that she was somewhere waiting and expecting him. He had seen Mr. Drayton; he was just the sort of man to behave as he had done, and it was quite terrible to think of that fair and innocent girl in his power.

He never rested till he got to Scotland. He went straight to Torbreck, where he interviewed the landlady. Miss Rivers had gone. She had gone to London to stay with her sister.

Sir Albert did not choose to say that her

sister was not there, but he made many minute inquiries about her health, and left Mrs. Munro much impressed by his manner, and the thoughtful remarks he made.

"He is a real bonny man," she said afterwards, "and, my certie, he kens how to put questions. He was as particular as he could be. Miss Rivers this and Miss Rivers that. She's a straight nose has Miss Rivers. I'm no denying it, but she does not follow it. Miss Margaret's a deal friendlier; weel-a-weel, its a' ordered for the best."

Mrs. Dorriman was much taken aback when once more Sir Albert was shown into the drawing-room at Renton. She was too timid not to be alarmed by the arrival of a man who had made no secret of his admiration for Margaret.

Did he know anything, and what did he know? Her expression was so distinctly interrogatory that he answered it, and advancing towards her, and not waiting for the usual conventional greeting, he said, "I know all,

Mrs. Dorriman; I have seen her—I have seen Margaret!"

"Ah!" said the poor little woman, with a deep sigh of relief.

"It has been cruel work," he said, passionately. "Why could you not have saved her?"

"I never knew till too late. How could I save her?" She spoke startled, and for a moment thinking that he was right. Then she remembered—"That unfortunate sister of hers, Grace, would not allow her to send for us. I did not know where she was. And when you left me, you gave me no address; even if I had had it I am not sure I should have written to you. It was then too late. Nothing could have been done. . . . How is Margaret?" she asked, after a moment's pause.

He did not answer her at once. Then he said in a broken voice, "I never saw any one so changed; she is only a shadow of her former self."

"God help her!" murmured Mrs. Dorriman.

"It has been terrible for us both," he said, hurriedly, in a tone he vainly endeavoured to make calm; "we will speak of it once and never again. She, poor darling, misunderstood something I said to her at Lornbay. It seems so strange to think that she did not see how I adored her. I was not free to speak to her quite openly, because when I was very young, little more than a schoolboy, I got into a foolish scrape, and my mother made me promise never to confess my love to any one without first letting her know it. She understood the word 'free' to mean that I was in some way bound to some one else. Her pride was in arms, and she seems to have fancied that she had not rightly understood me. You can imagine that such an idea worked together with her passionate wish to help Grace, and has ruined our happiness."

"God help her!" again ejaculated Mrs. Dorriman.

"All that I can now do is to work for her sister. Mr. Drayton refuses all help, and will not receive her, and Margaret is nearly frantic. I have been to Torbreck. She has gone from there."

"But where?" said Mrs. Dorriman. "You must not judge my brother hardly, Sir Albert, but, as Grace is at the bottom of poor Margaret's sacrifice, my brother would not have her here; he would not help her, understanding that Mr. Drayton had agreed to do so."

"And he refuses also. Well, my first business must be to find the poor girl, and yet, Mrs. Dorriman, I may do harm instead of good, if I make the search in person. Can you think of no one who would undertake it?"

Mrs. Dorriman thought in vain. She knew of no one, and she feared greatly for Grace, who had little money, no experience, and who was so self-willed—she would probably injure her health, already so delicate, by doing a thousand imprudent things.

"Let us ask Jean," she said, with a hasty explanation of her position; and Jean, summoned to give her advice, which she dearly loved doing—came upon the scene, the picture of an old Highland servant of the best type, full as much of respect as of self-respect.

"Jean," said Mrs. Dorriman, " Mrs. Drayton, Miss Margaret I mean, is anxious about her sister. She has left Torbreck, and we do not know where she has gone. I think you may help us. Do you know of any one she could go to in the South?"

"How is Miss Margaret? I cannot give her that other name yet," said Jean, addressing herself directly to Sir Albert Gerald.

"She is pretty well," he answered, absently; he was thinking of the pale face, and trusting that he might trace her sister, and bring a little comfort and happiness to her heart, and that the sad wistful look might be softened and cheered.

"Well, ma'am," said Jean, turning to Mrs. Dorriman, " as regards Miss Grace, I am inclined to think they will know where she is at the railway station here."

"The railway station? Has she been here?"

"No, ma'am, she has not been here, but she directed me to send her boxes there a while ago, and I did so; and it is my belief that once she was well, she's not long been parted from her boxes."

Sir Albert seized his hat, then he remembered that supposing they had her address, he must still arrange about some one communicating with her.

"If we find her address, what can we do next? I will, of course, take any trouble; but some one had better go, who might be of some use to her."

Mrs. Dorriman coloured. She had no means of her own, and she was not sure that her brother would furnish any; otherwise, she was quite prepared to go any distance, or do any thing she conceived to be helpful.

Sir Albert saw the hesitation, and he said, anxiously, "I hope whoever does undertake this errand of charity will allow me to help—in the only way in my power."

"Sir," said Jean, "we will allow you to help if we find help necessary. Mrs. Dorriman has plenty of everything to fall back upon if she needs it in that way. She does not trail about in velvet, but she has it if she wants it."

"Hush, Jean," said her mistress; "will you go yourself to the railway station and make inquiries, and Sir Albert will wait till you return, at any rate."

Jean obeyed, and Mrs. Dorriman, turning to the young man, said, with a heightened colour and a little pathetic gesture,

"It may seem strange to you, but, though I have everything I can possibly want given me by my brother, I have no command of money. You are no kin, only a friend, but somehow I do not feel it so hard to be beholden to you as I ought."

"Thank you for those words," he said, earnestly; "you will be doing me a very real service if you will use my money for this. It is the only thing I can do," he added sadly.

Jean soon returned from the station, wearing a little air of triumph.

"'Deed, and was I no just quite right?" she said; "Miss Grace sent for her things only yesterday, and I got the man to put the address down on paper for me: these uncanny English names are hard to mind on."

Mrs. Dorriman and Sir Albert read it together.

"The Limes, Wandsworth."

"Mr. Drayton's place," said Mrs. Dorriman; "how strange! and you are quite sure? he refused to allow her to go there."

She spoke in a lowered tone but Jean heard the words.

"That would not stop Miss Grace," she said, with a short laugh; "if she's minded to do anything she's not easy stopped."

Mrs. Dorriman thoughtfully passed the paper through her hands. How could she put the case before Mr. Sandford so as to win it?

Each time she spoke of either Grace or Margaret to him, he lost his temper, and created a scene that made her ill and nervous for days. If it would do good she would brave it, but if it did no good ——

Sir Albert watched her anxiously. He felt that, to be of real use to Grace, to *her* sister, there must be a womanly hand, and he saw that he was not sufficiently behind the scenes to appreciate all the difficulties of this kind, but timid woman.

He felt so more than ever when Mr. Sandford came in. He was in such a towering passion that he could hardly speak: he barely noticed Sir Albert, but threw himself into a chair and glared straight before him. He was in that phase of temper when a man is anxious to make all his belongings uncomfortable, and, if possible, put them out of temper also.

Sir Albert would have left, but Mrs. Dorriman saw that something worse than usual had happened; she was always frightened when her brother was with her alone, and when he was out of temper she was simply terrified. She made a gesture of entreaty, which checked the young man's impulse to go away.

There was a silence which fell like a terrible weight upon the two, who looked at each other unconscious of their mutual attraction, but the look was seen by the master of the house, and it set his passion alight. He sprang from his chair, he poured out a volley of abuse, upon his sister, Grace, and Margaret, swearing and using the most terrible language, reducing poor Mrs. Dorriman to a helpless state of terror and dismay.

Sir Albert looked at him with the most supreme astonishment. He now understood the whole thing; Grace had been exposed to this and she had gone, and he could not wonder at it. He could quite understand now that Margaret had felt any life was better than this. In his compassion for them he spoke aloud his thoughts.

"No wonder they fled from this," he said,

all unconsciously, as he looked at Mr. Sandford's wild gestures, with an overpowering sense of indignation.

Mr. Sandford heard him and understood. He turned round upon him, and said,

"You do not know what cause I have for anger; it is a just anger. The man who has married Margaret is a scoundrel and a swindler, and he is ruined, and he has nearly ruined *me?*"

Before another word could be spoken there was the sound of an arrival, and, while the three stood breathless, with all their emotions of rage and compassion, on either side, held for the moment in check, there glided into the room, her head as high as ever, but looking fatigued and troubled,—Grace Rivers!

"I have come back," she said, as she sank into a chair; "I am too tired just now to explain everything; and," turning to Mrs. Dorriman, "will somebody pay the cab, for I have no money."

There was a pause. Mr. Sandford's rage

had exhausted itself, fortunately for Grace, and she sat leaning back in her chair and surveying them all with a keen look of inquiry.

"I cannot enter into everything now, but I have been to Mr. Drayton's house; he has sold it, and I have come here because I have nowhere else to go."

CHAPTER V.

When Mr. Drayton returned on the day that Sir Albert had seen Margaret, he came home sorely put out. He had such a complete belief in himself that it annoyed him to find, as he did find every day, that the loss of his manager was in all ways a loss to him. Nothing seemed to prosper just now, and he was annoyed and very much harassed. Entering the little hotel where he had left Margaret, he asked if a man he had expected to call, had called.

The landlord, who was a stout, comfortable, little man, with a strong burr in his voice and a thickness, coming partly from natural guttural tendencies and partly from beer and pipes, answered in the negative, but he said that he thought the gracious lady had interviewed him in the garden.

Surprised, he went to his wife immediately and asked if this was true.

Margaret, who had resolved upon telling him that Sir Albert had been there, and who had spent much time since his departure in thinking whether she was bound to tell her husband what had passed, was taken by surprise, and a quick flush came into her usually pale face.

Like many fair and delicate-looking women she coloured vividly and the flush coloured her throat. Her husband watched her with a suspicious and angry frown, very different from the laughing, mocking one he usually showed her.

"Sir Albert Gerald passed this place accidentally," she said, "he did not know we were here. He spoke to me for a little while, then he went away."

"Indeed! and what makes you turn as red as a peony, because I found this out, eh?"

"You look so strange," she said, frightened a little by his manner.

"Do I? Do you suppose I can look pleased when I see that this man's visit has such power over your cold and indifferent nature, and that for him you tremble and blush, while for me —— ? Where is this man?" and he rose and went towards the door.

"He has gone to England," said Margaret, gently. "'He passed by the purest accident and saw me; he did not know that I was married. . . . He went away at once."

"Oh! and what did it matter to him whether you were married or unmarried?" he said, angrily; "was he your lover?"

"I never knew it till ——" Margaret was too truthful to shirk a direct question.

"Well, be good enough to speak; if you do not ——" and he moved close up to her.

His threat gave Margaret courage.

"I have no wish to hide anything from you," she said, coldly and with dignity; "I did not know that Sir Albert Gerald cared for me. I misunderstood something he said to me about not being free. He did not know where I was, and yesterday he passed by accident. He did not know anything. I told him I was now your wife and . . . ."

"And you have cried ever since he left, and that is why you grow white and red," he said. "Had you known he loved you would you have married me?"

"Never!" said Margaret, looking at him directly.

"Thank you," he said, "now I know you. I have been a fool all round!"

He threw himself into a chair and gazed moodily before him.

"You married me knowing I had no love to give," Margaret said, gently; "I told you myself."

"You did not tell me you loved some one else," he said savagely, "and that is quite different; you have deceived me from first to last!"

"I have never wilfully deceived you—and I did not know it myself," she said. "I thought it had been but a pleasant break in my life, and that all was over."

He made her no answer, but as he rose to leave the room he said, "You must be ready to start to-night after dinner. Some bad news hurries me to England."

"To England!" exclaimed Margaret, quickly. "Oh, I shall be glad to be at home once more."

He looked at her for a moment, and then, throwing his head back, he laughed in his usual loud way, and, for the first time, the sound brought relief to her.

She little knew him. She did not know the morbid intense jealousy that filled him. He never forgot the smallest slight to himself, or the tiniest wound offered to his vanity. He kept these feelings carefully covered up, but, sooner or later, he brought them forward, and if he could revenge himself, he did, when the whole transaction had been entirely forgotten by the delinquent himself.

Going to England meant being nearer Grace, from whom she had not heard for a long time, and she felt less forlorn and happier than she had done for a very long time.

Poor child! She did not recognise the great difference Sir Albert's words had made to her. She did not analyse her feelings, but she was really happier because the sting of having loved unsought was taken away from her. She did not realise how much this wounded and hurt her. Now the pain was lighter, all was easier to bear.

Margaret had never dwelt much upon the subject of her husband's wealth, and since he had broken faith with her, and had refused to help Grace, she had made up her mind that she would manage to do so—so soon as she had the command of money she expected to have, as a matter of course. She was one of the few women who not only did not care for ornament but who rather disliked it. She had a preference for everything simple and fresh, and considered that all things in the matter of dress were spoiled by ornamentation and trimming. She loved soft stuffs that took graceful folds, and had a dislike to rustling silks, and the few gowns she had, were remarkable for their softness, the harmonious colouring in which no two colours ever entered, and a certain fitness for her peculiar style. This outward expression of her sense of what was pleasant to look at, was in correspondence with her purity of thought, into which so little that was mean or small could enter. She might be what Grace always said she was —exalted and apt to incline to a certain exaggeration of feeling about all things; but everyday things to her seemed of importance, since they affected the lives of others, and she had the highest possible conception of the duties of life in general, and of her own life in particular. She resolutely put away from her all thoughts of what might have been, and resolved to do her best to be a more congenial wife to her husband. In order to fulfil these duties she must learn to know him better, to understand his affairs, and to show her interest in his occupations.

Mr. Drayton, who at this moment was guarding his losses and his real position carefully from the knowledge of every one as far as possible, was disagreeably surprised by her developing what he considered curiosity on the subject. He imagined directly that in some way she had received a hint, and was proportionately alarmed and annoyed.

He found it useless to try and give her superficial explanations, which were generally inconsistent. She was so completely unprejudiced, and her real interest lay so completely outside those things, that her critical faculty was utterly impaired, and she demonstrated his fallacies with a quickness which amazed him. She had all the acuteness he was wanting in, and he was forced to confess to himself that had it not been too late, she might have given him valuable help.

But he did not understand her, and he mistrusted her; consequently he gave her no real confidence, and indeed upon more than one occasion he tried to mislead her.

From that moment she never asked him another question. She had done what she conceived to be her duty, and the result was to lower him for ever in her eyes. She was indeed a severe young judge, as many of her discoveries were "in the way of business," and might have been made to bear an elastic interpretation; but she was conscious that this outcome of her sense of duty was destroying every chance of forbearing with her husband's peculiarities, and, if so, she must resign herself to not understanding; she gave him no more trouble, and he was equally incapable of comprehending the withdrawal of her interest as he was of its origin.

Without a soul to speak to, without any real interest in her life, Margaret did what many a woman before her has done, where there has existed an unusually active brain and no outlet for thought in any other direction. She began to write, and her sense of harmony, and the fervid and poetical temperament she possessed, drove her to writing in metre.

Not always. She sometimes wrote down her impressions of character, of scenes—she put down those rapid and subtle changes of feeling about things animate and inanimate that received life and colour from the mood of the moment. She found so great a relief from this occupation that it gradually absorbed her. It was like pouring out her very soul to a friend, who could never wound her or disappoint her.

But she never conceived that there was any danger in it. All was carefully destroyed or locked away. She had many lonely hours and a constant struggle with herself. But for this occupation she would have suffered more. The moment a passionate grief or sorrow can find expression it obtains relief, it is the being pent up and choked back that gives intensity.

She had known love (such as he required) to be impossible as regarded her husband, but she had thought esteem and a certain regard enhanced by his business ability, was within her reach. She now discovered that he was not true, that he had no great capacity or clearness of understanding, and that his standard in all and everything was as low as it could be.

This discovery was not so much a shock to her as an excuse for her not caring more for him. She had been guided by instinct to a right judgment of his character; and there was a sense of having understood him from the first, which was not without its gratification.

All this went down on paper—as a critical essay it was admirable, trenchant, concise, and to the point—but it was a terrible picture judged dispassionately, and, as Margaret finished it, she hastily put it into her blotting-book; she felt troubled and guilty when her husband called her, and she resolved to destroy this record of her inmost convictions. She had perhaps been wrong in writing it, even for her own eye. Then they left that evening.

The journey was hurried over with small regard to her comfort and convenience, but Margaret heeded nothing; the thoughts of once more being within reach of Grace supported her through fatigue and all else.

She was quite aware as regarded her husband that had she chosen to flatter him, and had she only been able to stoop a little, she might have ruled him, but her principle was too high for this, and she made a point of being honest with him to her own loss.

When they reached London it was yet early in the morning, and they went, greatly to her surprise, to a small and very second-rate hotel in the City, where everything was dingy and mean.

"Are we not going home?" Margaret asked, astonished.

Mr. Drayton laughed uneasily.

"The truth is that there are some people in my house."

"Oh! it is let," said Margaret, in a tone of disappointment. "Then what are we to do?"

"We might take lodgings—they must not be far from here, and then we can see ——" He turned on his heel and left her.

When she had rested, she started in a cab to look for lodgings—a weary quest—and all she saw near that part of London were so dingy and so dirty that she returned to the hotel in despair. Her husband came in looking so white and so utterly broken down that she could not imagine what had happened; but he would tell her nothing.

The landlady to whom Margaret spoke suggested some rooms in the country close to a station.

"As you think so much of cleanliness and fresh air, you had better go there, ma'm."

"It is only for a little while—my husband

let his place and cannot turn out his tenants before their time is up," said Margaret, happily unconscious what a falsehood this was.

She liked the rooms; and then, when they paid their bill and were leaving, her husband made her understand a little how things were.

Throwing a handful of silver on the table he exclaimed, angrily,

"There! that is every penny I have in the world."

Margaret stared at him—want of money had never yet presented itself to her in connection with him. She did not now understand him literally, but she was startled.

That evening, cheered by the bright cleanliness of the little cottage at Chiselhurst to which they had removed, she asked him to tell her what was wrong.

Then he told her.

"I have lost everything!" he said. "I have not a shilling in the world left, except that money settled upon you. I am ruined— I do not suppose I shall have anything to live upon at all," and he laid his head upon his arms and cried like a child.

"Is there nothing I can do?" faltered Margaret.

"Yes!" he said. "You can go away, Mr. Sandford will take you—you can go. Our married life has been a short, if it has not been a merry, one," he said, bitterly, and he burst into a laugh so wild that Margaret left the room.

She wrote a long letter to Mr. Sandford; understanding him too well to appeal to him for assistance, she asked him to come and look into everything.

"I know a little of my husband's affairs, very little, but what I know convinces me that all cannot be so completely lost as he thinks; I fancy that, unduly elated at times, he is just now unduly depressed; and your clear brain will unravel much—besides, my husband is not well."

This invitation followed Grace's abrupt appearance at his house; and Mr. Sandford, who was, to a certain extent, involved in Mr. Drayton's fall, was content to obey the summons; more than content, there was much that required explanation, and it was a temptation he could not resist.

He was also pleased to have an opportunity of consulting a good doctor about himself. He was unwell and irritable even beyond his normal irritability; and felt ill and completely out of sorts when Mrs. Dorriman met him at breakfast, with a speech carefully arranged to do Grace good and avoid hurting his susceptibilities; she found the question of Grace's remaining in his house had sunk into a question of little importance, and that her little speech, like many another, was not required.

He left Renton, soothed by Margaret's letter to him, and full of bringing her back with him. Of course she would leave Drayton, now he could no longer support her, and he should have her again. Grace he never remembered.

When that young lady woke in the morning

she felt surprised to hear all so quiet, and, ringing her bell, she asked Jean, who answered the bell, why all was so still, " Is every body dead and buried ? " she said, laughing.

"Eh ! Miss Grace, we was to keep quiet for you ; you looked so ill last night, Mrs. Dorriman and I have been saying 'whisht!' all the morning, to let you sleep. Shall I bring you some tea ? "

"If you will," said Grace ; her tone was indifferent, but Jean saw that her eyes had a wistful look in them.

"What is it, my bairn ? " the old woman said, her kind heart warming towards the poor girl, so evidently hovering at the gates of death.

" It is nothing," said Grace, with a pitiful little laugh, " but no one has offered to do any thing for me for a long while."

Jean understood, and, when she took in the tea, Mrs. Dorriman accompanied her.

Some women are distinctly born with a gift

for nursing, and Mrs. Dorriman was one of these women. Grace, weak and feeble, worn out by the journey, the want of rest and comfort of the last few weeks, was nursed as few are nursed.

She was too weak to wonder about anything. She never asked for Mr. Sandford, and only once for Margaret. She lay there in the place she had so hated, grateful now for its shelter.

She touched lightly upon her experiences during that interval when she had left Torbreck, and had gone to London to see the world, and Mrs. Dorriman was too wise to question her.

Mr. Sandford only wrote once, and that was a short note to his sister, "Margaret refuses to leave her husband," he said, "so you need not expect her."

"I never thought she would," murmured Mrs. Dorriman to herself, to whom it had never occurred as possible.

At Chislehurst, in the small place called by courtesy a villa, Margaret had at first to face her husband's anger. Nothing could have been more hateful to him than this inquiry into his affairs Margaret had requested Mr. Sandford to make, and yet he had no reason to give against it, and it was natural that Mr. Sandford should act for Margaret.

Grace's return was a fresh and a most painful surprise for Margaret. She realised now that she might have saved herself; if Grace could of her own free-will seek shelter at Mr. Sandford's hands, she might have been urged to do so before, and so her sacrifice might have been unnecessary—might? would have been. But once this reflection was fought with, she was glad that her sister, still so delicate, was with Mrs. Dorriman.

In the meantime Mr. Sandford and his unwilling assistant, Mr. Drayton, waded through a mass of papers and accounts; and various transactions came to light that reflected no credit on Mr. Drayton's ability, and still less on his honesty. Some of his acts had been bad, and some were the action of a madman;

and were to Mr. Sandford's cool Scotch caution and clear head utterly incomprehensible. He made few remarks, however, betraying his sentiments only by a secret and sudden clench of his hand, as though it might be a relief to knock down something or somebody.

It was so difficult, also, to get at the exact truth of anything; there were endless memorandums but nothing to tell what these referred to—a contemplated purchase or to one completed.

When all was known, things were better than Mr. Drayton had at first feared, in so far that a few hundreds a year were left him, but only that.

Mr. Sandford had an interview with Margaret; he thought her looking ill, and he wanted her to go to Scotlaad with him, to see Grace. She referred to her husband, and asked him if he would mind her going.

"Mind it! Will that matter?" he said, curtly.

"I wish to go if you can spare me," she said gently.

"I can spare you," he said, very roughly; "if you wish to go, that is quite sufficient."

"I wish to see my sister. I will not stay away long; and whilst I am away will you not arrange something? Are you going to sell your house—you like it, I know, and the garden?"

She spoke, wishing to cheer him. Mr. Sandford had told her that he was not obliged to sell this place. She did not quite understand her husband's remaining so downcast, and in such an odd state, and she was vexed that Mr. Sandford should see him in so disagreeable a light.

After some discussion it was agreed that he should go to the Limes, and have everything put in order for his wife's return. But as they parted she caught his expression, and it made her so uncomfortable that she felt vexed at having left him just then.

This impression left her after a little while,

she sat very silent all the long journey, and Mr. Sandford had on his side much to think of.

When they arrived at Renton, Grace was in a state of excitement almost painful to witness. She laughed, she cried, she moved about her, till Margaret persuaded her to be quiet and to go to bed. She feared all manner of things she hardly knew what; and, longing for rest and quiet herself, she felt most thankful that Mrs. Dorriman had given her another room. Next day she found she had still a battle to fight with Mr. Sandford.

"Now your husband is not in a position to do anything for your sister," he said, "you will stay here."

"Stay for a time, yes, but my husband's losses will make him wish to have me with him more than ever, I think. He did not wish me to stay away?"

"Oh! he wants you fast enough, but you cannot pretend to care for him; and, now that he has been such a fool as to squander a magnificent fortune, what can your object be in going back to him?"

"To do my duty," said Margaret, simply.

"Your duty! To my thinking, as he has not behaved at all well, you are not bound to go back to him. Has he behaved well? I ask you plainly."

Margaret did not answer the question.

"Nothing can absolve me from doing what I feel to be right."

She spoke very quietly, and Mr. Sandford said no more at the time, but he constantly renewed the subject, and Margaret was weary of repeating her own views of her position.

It was hard enough to find him so bent upon her staying, it was harder still to parry the urgent attacks made by her sister.

"If you go I shall die," Grace said one day, after a long and weary argument, in which poor Margaret had tried to show her a higher sense of duty.

"Why do you try me so?" Margaret said at length. "Can you never see things seriously? Oh, Grace, can you conceive it possible for me to take a solemn vow and make light of it afterwards?"

"But you cannot pretend that you *love* that man, Margaret?"

"Therein lies my sin—and my punishment," the young wife answered with a quivering lip. "We cannot command our affections—that I know, but we can check them, and we can at any rate try and not fail in other things."

Grace did not like the grave tone she spoke in; she had rallied from the fatigue of her journey, and amused her sister often by her endeavours to win a smile from Mr. Sandford. She was as usual reckless in her speech, and the only difference Margaret could see was that she did not try to provoke him; on the contrary, in all her sallies now, there was a certain subtle implied deference to his wishes, new and rather winning.

The same sad reflection came often to Margaret. Seeing Grace so contented now, she quite forgot her misery at the prospect of such a home before her; and she was forced to see that she had ruined her own life on insufficient grounds. There was so much pain in this, and Grace's wild spirits so jarred upon her, that after a few days had passed away she announced her departure.

It was only then that she found how Grace clung to the idea of going with her.

"Why cannot I go with you? Surely Mr. Drayton cannot be so barbarous as to separate us now."

"I do not know what arrangements he has been able to make, dear. I must go alone, first."

"If you go alone I shall never follow: I know so well what it will be."

"I will do my best; surely you know that I will do my best; you know it is my dearest wish."

"Yes, but you know, my dear old thing, that you have *not* got my power of managing people. Now look at old Sandford. Swore I should never live here again: anathematized me, I believe, and sent his poor little sister into fits, such was the violence of his language, and, after all this, I return; I walk in. I am no hypocrite, and I say quite quietly that I only came because I had nowhere else to go, —and the lion became a lamb."

"You do not understand Mr. Drayton."

"Is he worse than the old bear here?" and Grace made a comical face of dismay.

Margaret did not smile. She forced herself to speak plainly.

"It is difficult to know what is right sometimes," she said, thoughtfully. "I never could tell an untruth, and sometimes telling the truth does not make things smooth. Grace, my darling, I married Mr. Drayton to give you a home and comforts you so sorely needed. He knows it was *only* for that, and he resents it, and he will *never* let me have you, never."

She sobbed, and she was not given to tears.

Grace stared at her in stupefied astonishment.

"You do not mean to say that you let him find this out?"

"No, I told him. I told him before I married him. How could I act a lie?"

"And he married you after this frank explanation, and now turns round upon you! How like a man!" and Grace, who had a most limited acquaintance herself with any men, looked supremely scornful. "Well, my dear Margaret, I shall not go with you, but I shall follow you."

"But Grace, darling ——"

"But Margaret, darling. I will not hear a single word. I shall choose my own time and arrive in my own way—but go I will."

She laughed Margaret's scruples to scorn and turned the subject.

Grace was so gay and bright, so overflowing with good-humour, that all the inmates of Renton Place were taken by surprise, save and except Jean, who answered Mrs. Dorriman's expression of satisfaction by one short sentence,

"Milk aye bubbles before it boils."

And Mrs. Dorriman felt angry, and accused her faithful old servant of prejudice and superstition, to which Jean made not the slightest reply.

Margaret was a little uneasy; her experience of Grace's wilfulness made her dread some step that would bring happiness to neither of them. But she heard no more of her projected visit, and by degrees she began to hope that it had merely been a wild way of talking.

One great change was brought about by her sister's delicacy. Mr. Sandford, talking to the doctor one day about himself—Grace refused to see any doctor there—alluded to the eldest Miss Rivers as being delicate.

"We can never get her to go out; she says it tires her; she was always indolent."

"Or delicate," said the doctor; "she should not tire herself; you should send her out driving."

"Out driving! Why there is no carriage."

"No reason there should not be," said the doctor, pleasantly.

The new idea rather took possession of Mr. Sandford, and before many days were over Grace was told that she was to go out, and that a carriage was at her service.

Mr. Sandford's gruff way of announcing this fact did not prevent her seeing the real kindness, and she thanked him, while tears glistened in her eyes and she had a jest on her lips.

Margaret saw her revive under the influence of the fresh air. She had more than once postponed her journey, greatly against her own wishes, and yielding only to Grace's urgent prayers. At length she left Renton, with a heavy heart for her sister. She had too great an affection for her not to see that the excitement and gay manner were all, in reality, part of her illness; she dreaded the worst; each time she tried to talk to her seriously Grace either laughed her to scorn or cried till she made herself ill, and no good was done.

As she went south she tried to face the

duties that awaited her—to remember only that her husband was her husband.

It was late and dark when she arrived in London, and when she got to Wandsworth she tried in vain to make out her surroundings. She could see nothing but the lamp-posts; and the scanty light the lamps gave, and which spread such a little distance, served to make the gloom between them darker.

She arrived at length at the Limes, so called because a couple of lopped lime-trees stood sentinel on either side of the gate.

No one was there at the door to meet her. At length an untidy-looking woman arrived—seemed surprised to see her — waited with visible impatience whilst she paid the cabman, dragged in the slender luggage and banged the gate, showing young Mrs. Drayton the way up a flagged footway between some straggling laurels, and into a cheerless unfurnished little stone hall.

"Is Mr. Drayton here? Did he not expect

me?" asked the poor young wife, her heart sinking within her.

"Oh! Mr. Drayton's there. He said nothing of your being expected."

She opened a door, and sitting in front of a table littered with papers sat her husband, his face buried in his hands.

He looked at her with a vacant smile—he did not know her.

He was terrible to look at, so unkempt and so neglected looking. He must be ill, very ill!

The fire was out and the room undusted and unswept, a close smell she did not recognise filled the room.

She persuaded him to lie down on the sofa; she got the fire lit; threw open the window, put on the kettle for hot water, and wrote a note, which she sent by the woman to the nearest doctor.

He came and looked down upon the prostrate figure.

Is he very ill?" asked Margaret, anxiously.

"No, madam," he answered, with a strange expression on his face, " he is only very drunk."

CHAPTER VI.

Margaret stared at the doctor, who so calmly announced this appalling fact to her, with widely opened eyes and a blanched face.

Ignorant of her history, he was startled to find so young a creature in such a position, and he said, impelled to respect by her whole air and manner, "This is news, and very unwelcome news, to you?"

"I have this moment arrived from nursing my sister in Scotland," she said, hurriedly. "My husband has been alone... All is very wretched; can you tell me where I could hear of a nurse, I suppose, and—servants?"

"You must have a male nurse," he said.

"I will send you in a man-servant I know of, and to-morrow things will be better." He stayed with her a little while, lost in astonishment over her beauty, her grace, and the extraordinary contrast existing between her and the man she called her husband.

"I shall be afraid—to-night. He might be ill."

"Oh! you must not be left alone with him," he answered, and then, noting her weariness and pallor, he said, "If you will go and have some refreshment I can wait here, and when I leave I will send you some one."

She thanked him, and went to see if there was any room she could take possession of. To her relief the rooms upstairs were all furnished; and when she had bathed her face and had some slight refreshment she went downstairs again.

"I may tell you that my own conviction is that this terrible business is not a habit," said the doctor, as she entered. "Mr. ——" looking at her for the name which she supplied, "has not any of the signs of an habitual drunkard. He has had something now which has had a terrible effect upon him; when that effect is over he will perhaps never relapse. Of course, I speak from imperfect knowledge, but I think I am right."

Poor Margaret could not answer him. She saw him go with a feeling akin to despair. She sat looking at the fire, and then at the man she had vowed to honour—and obey.

She rose hurriedly from her seat and rushed to the open window, suffocating with the agony and horror of it all. Was this to be her life?

She had sinned, and this was her punishment; and she was so young, so very young. She had, perhaps, a long life before her. How she shrank from this prospect, and from another confronting her then. Tears came; and kneeling before the window she allowed them to fall. Never was any girl more wretched, never was any more forlorn, than this poor child; helpless, lovely, and endowed with many gifts she was as yet all unconscious of.

She was roused by a man's step on the pavement leading to the house. She had not heard him ring, but he entered; a stern, grave man, with eyes accustomed to control the weak will of others, accustomed to see scenes far worse than this—far more terrible.

He asked to be shown Mr. Drayton's bedroom, and then he turned to Mrs. Drayton, who stood still watching: "You can sleep without anxiety, madam," he said, respectfully; "I will look after this poor gentleman." And Margaret thanked him, and fled to her own room, where she locked herself in and wept and prayed by turns, and finally slept.

The sun shone brightly into her room next day, when she opened her weary eyes in all the dim consciousness of a heavy trial awaiting her.

She rang, and had her breakfast brought upstairs (such as it was), and her luggage.

The Limes was a pretty place — large for a suburban villa. There was an extensive lawn behind, and flower-beds; but beyond the shrubbery, and all round the place, was a high brick wall, on the top of which, in spite of a height which seemed to forbid such a possibility, was a quantity of broken glass to keep out intruders. This wall destroyed all Margaret's happiness, she thought it made the place seem like a prison.

She dressed and went downstairs, and was met by the man who had come in the previous evening. Mr. Drayton was better, but it was wiser not to see him just yet, he said, firmly but respectfully; and poor Margaret felt afraid he might see too plainly upon her face that this prohibition was a relief.

When the doctor called, which he did soon, he told her he had been asked by his wife to say she would gladly be of use, and could recommend servants: and all that day she was busy seeing them and arranging matters a little.

In a few days her husband walked into the dining-room; greeted her laughingly, as though she had only just returned; and was apparently as well as ever.

But she noticed that the man-servant, who had replaced the first person, paid no attention to him when he called for wine, and that he provided him with a weak dilution from the side-board.

The days passed on in monotonous regularity, Margaret's happiness consisting of not seeing her husband; her misery, when she did. She got books and read, and she cultivated her flowers; and tried to resign herself to her life. But it was impossible for her fervent and passionate nature to be resigned. Though she had herself put on this yoke, her anguish was no less.

She often tormented herself by wondering whether love would have outlived this terrible experience; surely the sincerest love would have received its death-blow.

Some months had passed when Margaret lived through a time in which death seemed very close at hand, and had her baby in her arms. She had not looked forward to this happily, but when it came, all motherhood awoke in her nature; all her love, pent up, and finding no outlet in another direction, flowed to this helpless and feeble creature. She lavished endless caresses upon it; she lived for it; she worshipped it.

Her letters to Grace, so scanty and so bare of any information, were now full of her infant, its progress, and its wonderful intelligence.

Mr. Drayton showed no feeling but that of jealousy in connection with it; but Margaret did not mind. It slept in her room, and she devoted herself to it.

Up to this time Mr. Drayton had never again given her cause for fearing him.

Even the experienced servant pronounced him as well as any one, and he resumed his usual occupations.

One night Margaret was upstairs with her child—late.

There had been a thunder-storm, and the thunder was still growling in the distance. Rain came on, and as Margaret sat by her little one she felt only natural pity for any wayfarers on such a stormy night.

How it poured, and how dark the night was! She closed the shutters for fear of the baby's slumbers being disturbed by the loud splashing of the rain upon a lower roof of an outhouse, and was taking up her book again, when her husband walked into the room, looking perfectly wild, a paper in his hand. With great difficulty she got him to go down stairs with her, calling her nurse to go to the child.

Cautious, and seeing how frightfully excited he was, she sat down near the bell, and tried to speak to him quietly.

But she was frightened when she saw that the paper he held was the record of her opinion of his character, written in Germany—that she had meant to destroy, and had long forgotten.

"So, madam," her husband said furiously, "this is your candid opinion of me." He spoke in a tone of concentrated rage.

"It was written long ago," faltered Margaret.

"Oh, it was written long ago. Well, now I know your opinion of me I shall alter my conduct towards you—you sneaking . . . ."

He came towards her. Margaret, frightened, rang the bell, and the sound was to her surprise repeated outside. There was a commotion in the hall. Before she could speak Grace, wet, wearied, but with all her accustomed nonchalance, stepped into the room.

Before the sisters could clasp each other Mr. Drayton rushed between them furious. The sight of Grace, whom he hated, drove him to frenzy, and the servant entreated her to go, as he did his utmost to restrain him.

"Yes, you had better go, darling," sobbed Margaret.

"But you will not remain here, you will come too," pleaded Grace, panting.

"Oh, Grace, my child! I cannot leave it—I cannot risk moving it."

She wrote the doctor's address in pencil, and

saw her sister go, resolved that she would go and see her the next morning.

"The doctor will help you, Grace, and if you get some nice rooms I will manage for you."

She saw the frail figure in the cab, and, struck by the forlornness of her departure, she sent a servant with her. Then she went up stairs, and carefully locking the door tried to face this new and terrible complication.

What was she to do?

For the first time now she was really frightened. Her husband's expression had been so full of malice. How could she go on living in this way?

She thought long and deeply about it, and resolved that next day she would take baby to see Grace, leave it with her, and go and consult some clever lawyer as to what was possible for her to do. In her ignorance and inexperience she thought that the fact of his drinking would free her. She had yet much to learn.

Next day Mr. Drayton was not out of his room, and the discreet man-servant advised her to make haste and go out before he was up.

"He has been very troublesome and violent," he said, "and you had better not see him. He's got a turn against you just now, and how he got anything completely passes me. I have been watching him like a cat."

In a short time Margaret, with her nurse and baby, went off to see Grace, and much to her annoyance did not find her alone. Paul Lyons was there, full of sympathy, but sympathy expressed with very little tact; and while wishing to be a real friend—indeed, longing to hold that position—he wounded Margaret's pride by the way in which he allowed himself to speak to her of her husband.

She carried her point, however, and taking the train to London she went to a lawyer she had heard of, knowing no one herself. Her visit there was productive of no comfort to her.

Mr. Spratt was a busy man, and looked upon

all feminine clients in the light of obstructions. This one was very pretty, but an obstructionist nevertheless.

"How can I serve you, madam?" were his first words, and Margaret did not quite know how to state her case.

She looked at him for some moments, and his patience, not very unnaturally, began to give way. He wore blue spectacles, a circumstance which reduced every one to the same hue as regarded complexion, which was at the same time a drawback and a safeguard. Impelled to speak by his evident impatience, Margaret asked him with a trembling voice, "If a man drinks, can a wife leave him?"

"By mutual consent. If he illtreats her she can perhaps do so—by arrangement. Madam," he said, softening a little – a very little—at the soft pleading tones of her voice, "all you say to me is confidential—state your own, and not an abstract case. Does your husband drink?"

"Yes," said poor Margaret.

"Does he illtreat you when he is drunk?"

"No," said the poor child, trembling—"he—he frightens me."

"Ah! you see the law recognizes cruelty, and another thing, as a cause for legal separation, or even a divorce, but the fact of a man's being a drunkard is not taken into account."

"Not taken into account?" said Margaret, repeating his words in strongest surprise.

"No. So little does this fact—a very terrible fact—tell against a man in the eyes of the law, that, though you are too young to have children, *supposing* you had children, and that you left the father, the law gives the children to him and not to you—they remain with him, they do not go with you."

"God help me!" she murmured, fervently, her heart standing still in the great shock of this announcement. And if she had left him, as she had once thought of doing, her baby might have been kept from her.

"Then you cannot help me!"

"I am afraid not," he said, not unkindly; "the law as regards the rights of mothers is a little one-sided—a little unjust, I allow, but till they are altered —— "

"Good-bye," said Margaret, seized now with a sort of terror, lest something should have happened to her infant during her absence—she felt so far from it, she must hurry back.

"Good-bye, madam," said the old lawyer, seeing before him somebody not usual in his experience. "If your husband ever strikes you we might have a case."

"And my baby!"

"Good gracious—a baby! You have an infant? you look so very young," he said, in a tone of apology. "Ah, well, you see, we need not go into that question just now."

She went down stairs utterly broken down. She had always clung to a belief that if things got very bad she would be able to go. She had had a sort of blind belief that the laws of her country—boasted of so often, and the outcome of so much intellect and ability—were there to fall back upon and to protect her.

She stopped to take breath and gather herself together for a moment, and she was just moving away from the door when some one passed in a hansom,—in another moment he had pulled up short, jumped out, and dismissed the cabman. Then he was beside her, and in the moment of her deepest anguish Sir Albert Gerald stood beside her.

She was utterly miserable, too much crushed to feel surprised. He saw that she was quite unfit to be spoken to, that she had sustained some great shock, and he tried to think rapidly what was best for her.

"I wish to go back to my sister," she said at length in a low voice. "Will you take me there?"

He called a cab and put her into it, and got in and told the man to drive to the station.

What was the meaning of all this? She said her sister, not her husband. Had she left her husband? He was longing to know all, and yet he could not ask her anything.

"You know you can depend upon my friendship," he said earnestly to her, and the kindness of his tone, the care he took of her, everything contrasted with the misery of her home, and she lay back in the railway carriage with great tears unconsciously rolling over her face. He saw her safe to her sister's door, and there he left her, anxious not to increase her difficulties, but determined to be at hand should she require help.

"Here is my address," he said, as he gave it to her. "At any moment I am ready to serve you, and I trust and hope you will not refuse me this one thing left for me to do—let me be of some use to you."

"Thank you," said Margaret, gratefully. "If I go for help to any one I will go to you." And as she left him her smile of perfect confidence went to his heart.

Grace could not understand her sister's wild rapture when she once more held her baby in her arms. "I nearly lost you, oh, my darling!" she heard her murmur, and she lavished endearments upon it; and she seemed to hear nothing, see nothing, but it.

"A round chubby-faced baby, with no particular anything to distinguish it from other babies," was Grace's way of putting it.

Margaret had sustained so severe a shock that she was neither pleased nor displeased when Mr. Lyons appeared again, ready and anxious to walk to the Limes to see her home, and to try and have leave to call upon her.

As they drew near the place, however, Mr. Drayton was on the step (with his servant) looking out for his wife.

He was horribly afraid she had gone, and now that he was himself again he could not remember what had passed. His servant could not or would not remind him of anything, and the vague feeling of fright at having said or done something terribly violent, filled him with dread. But all these remorseful feelings were swept away when he saw Mr. Paul Lyons as her escort, the nurse and baby bringing up the rear.

She turned abruptly when she came up to him, and, as he slammed the heavy gate behind the small party who entered, a thrill of fear passed through poor Margaret's heart.

She felt as though a prison door had closed upon her.

Alas! could she have looked forward and seen the real future lying before her, how far, far deeper had been her anguish — how agonized her feelings!

She went up stairs with her baby. She had seen her husband turn into his sitting-room down stairs, and she stayed till dinner was ready, then she met him.

He was silent and sullen during dinner, and she tried in vain to get him to speak.

It was a dismal meal. Margaret was tired by her unwonted exertions, and frightfully depressed by the news she had heard, and Mr. Drayton was jealous and miserable and full of plans of vindictive revenge, his wife's written opinion of him rankling in his heart.

Next day fresh complications arose. Grace

sent her sister a note asking her if she could pay for the attendant and various luxuries she had had. "I don't think I told you that I had a violent tiff with old Sandford when I left him, so of course I cannot ask him for money. Will you send it to me to-day, please?"

Margaret had spent the very little she had in her yesterday's expedition; but she thought, though her husband would not have her sister in the house that he would not mind helping her. He had been generous enough when they were at Torbreck.

"Will you please give me a cheque?" she said to him when they met.

"What for?"

"I want to pay some things for my sister. You will not allow her to come here. She is not well enough to go back to Scotland. She wants the money."

"Does she?" he said. "Then she may want it! Not one single farthing of my money shall she have, that I swear!" and he thumped his hand down upon the table with violence.

"What am I to do?" asked his wife, in a tone of distress.

"What do I care? I feed and clothe you because you are my wife. I told you before I have not married your sister, and I will have nothing to do with her."

"I must go and see her, then, and make some arrangement for her," said Margaret, turning away.

"Not so fast," he said, while a laugh rang through the room that made her shiver again. "You do not go out again without *me*. I can tell you I am not going to allow a wretched stick of a fellow to run about with my wife any more—no, no!"

For one second, fear lest Sir Albert's escort should have been known to him—in itself so innocent, but perhaps she now thought imprudent—she coloured a little, and he noticed it, and it increased his rage.

"Mr. Lyons never shall have the pleasure of escorting you again," he said. "I will take care of that. Darby and Joan—Darby and

Joan!" and another wild burst of laughter rang out.

Margaret left him to think over her next step, and to send Grace a few lines to account for her non-appearance. She resolved to write to Mrs. Dorriman, and to lay before her something of her sad position. The whole truth she could not bring herself to put down.

But time went on; she got no letter from Grace nor from Mrs. Dorriman. Her husband seemed to spend his whole time in watching her, and if she attempted to go out he was beside her. She appealed to the man-servant, but he told her he was only there to see that her husband did not go out alone, and did not drink, for nothing else; that he could not interfere. "I cannot aid and abet you, madam," he said; "it *may* be your sister, again it may not be, and if something comes of it, it will not look well for *me*."

Margaret's indignant young face quelled him, and he stopped short.

She was perfectly helpless. She could

wander in the grounds, and see little of her husband. She could spend hours with her child, but she never could go out. She felt that this was indeed a prison, and she a prisoner!

She had not even the comfort of knowing that Grace had got her letters, since she received no answer; then she was terrified lest Grace should write and say something in her letter about Mr. Drayton.

She was utterly wretched about her; her nurse was a timid woman, and she had had one rebuff; she was afraid of altering her position towards her, and altogether the poor thing did not know what to do.

She was standing near the front door watching her baby go out into the garden when the front door bell rang violently, so loudly as to make her start. Before it could be opened the key had to be obtained from Mr. Drayton. When it was answered, Margaret, who had paused a little from curiosity, waited to see who could come to this sad and forlorn place.

To her amazement she saw Sir Albert

Gerald. He saw her, and before any conventional denial could be given he sprang forward and greeted her joyfully.

She was so overwhelmed with joy now that a friendly face appeared that she forgot everything but that she saw before her one who would go for her to her sister. She clung to his hand and led him into the sitting-room, where her husband, with angry eyes, was watching her.

But he said nothing; he rose and gave his hand, and a new fear came upon Margaret. If Mr. Drayton could so control himself, was there not cunning present? She knew that he drank. Now she feared he was mad. A remembrance of her earliest instinct against him came to her, and she covered her face with her hands. She could not say a word to Sir Albert without his hearing it, and she felt so thankful to him for keeping Mr. Drayton in conversation; it gave her time to think.

Abruptly then, she spoke of her sister, and begged him to go and see her, to let her know how she was. "You are a friend," she said; "you will see if you can help her. I cannot go and see her just now, much as I long to do so!"

Tears came into her eyes; he was shocked and frightened for her. There was something sinister in Mr. Drayton's expression.

He stayed as long as he could, and then he left, promising to return; and he left Margaret happier because of his promise to see her sister.

Mr. Drayton began to move restlessly about the room after Sir Albert's departure, and came suddenly close up to his wife; looking at her with a malicious smile, he said, "You shall *never* speak to another man so long as I live!" Margaret did not answer, but she rang the bell, and left him muttering to himself vengeance upon her and her visitor.

Sir Albert, meanwhile, went to Grace's lodgings, to find her ill, nervous, and most anxious about poor Margaret. She had no comforts about her and no proper attendance;

and seeing how really ill she was, and with poor Margaret full in his mind, he telegraphed to Mrs. Dorriman, and entreated her to lose no time, but to come south.

Next day he went to see Grace, and found her in one of her most excited moods, her eyes sparkling, her colour high.

She was at one moment making fun of everything, the next dwelling upon their own history.

She was full of remorse about Margaret. "It is so dreadful; I drove her to it—it is like a murder."

"I never understood it," Sir Albert said, in a low voice.

"Of course not. Poor darling! when he first proposed to her we were at Renton, and oh, it was hateful to me then, though I think it tolerable now; and I was wild to get away —anywhere from that smoky place. Poor Margaret refused him, and told me about it. . . . You will see why I am so heart-broken now. I was disappointed. I was so selfish, and I thought she might have done it."

" Is that when —— "

" Now, do not interrupt me," she said, struggling to speak in a light tone, though her heart was heavy. " I am just like a clock, I can go on when I am wound up, and if I am put back I strike all wrong."

" I will not interrupt you—but," he said, colouring, " would your sister wish me to hear all this—think only of her—if she disliked it ? "

" I am not thinking or talking of her, except with reference to my part of the story," said Grace, pettishly.

" Well, we went to Lornbay, I daresay you remember the place well, as you were laid-up there. Well, Margaret had another lover there " (she did not see him start), " and this long, lanky, would-be fast youth also wished to marry my Margaret, and, of course, she said, No ; and I was not at all annoyed," she continued, naïvely, " for he had not a sixpence.

"Well—you see I begin all my sentences with that useful word—but it was anything but well now. We went off to a most detestable little village called Torbreck, and there I stupidly caught cold and coughed. I never heard of any one who coughed as I did. Then Mr. Drayton found us out, and I forget exactly what he did, but he gave us ever so many things, and grapes; and how I thanked him. Then he again wanted to marry Margaret. Oh!" she exclaimed, the tears running down her face, "I never, never can forget one night. She came and knelt beside my bed, and she asked me if this sacrifice would really be what I wished; she said it would be giving her life, and that it was worse for her now than it had been before she had been at Lornbay. Sir Albert, do not turn away from me now. You cannot hate my deed worse than I do—you cannot have a lower opinion of me than I have of myself. I excited myself, and I bid her do it!" and Grace lay back in her chair utterly exhausted.

What could the young man say? The deed was done and nothing could undo it. The utter selfishness of Grace's conduct could find no excuse; he tried to master his emotion; he could only succeed in saying in a broken voice something about God's forgiveness.

But Grace was past all the anguish of seeing this horror in his face. She had exerted herself to tell him the story, and put Margaret right in his eyes; and she had given way to exhaustion, and was deaf and blind to all that passed round her—for the time.

He stayed a little while, and left her, shocked at the violence of his own feeling against her.

The image of his poor childish love—kneeling beside the bedside of the sister she adored, who sacrificed her remorselessly—for what? A few luxuries.

It was absolutely terrible to think of, and he forgot to take into account the feebleness of health that might have impaired judgment. He waited in London till he thought Mrs. Dorriman had time to answer, whence for fear of any mistakes he had dated his telegram. Her answer came, and was not fully satisfactory. *My brother is very ill, and I cannot leave him, but I send my maid Jean.*

He went again to Grace's lodgings, and he told the landlady that an old family servant was on her way. Then he tried to think how best to convey this news to Margaret.

He felt that his having been admitted was a chance, and he was afraid of making things worse for her by going there too often; but he must risk something, she must know in some way about her sister, she must have her mind set at rest.

Unable to make up his mind he was wandering about when he was attracted by a curious-looking book in a bookseller's shop. It was something more than a shop, for he read there that it was no less a place than the office of the "Industrious Workman," a paper he knew by name.

He went in to ask the price of the book, and the intelligent little man, who was tearfully reading a poem, put it down to attend to him, saying as he did so, " I beg pardon for being so absorbed, but I have something very lovely here;" and handing him the paper Sir Albert recognised in the neatly-written lines—Margaret's handwriting.

CHAPTER VII.

When Margaret left Renton Place, and that Grace had seen her off, the first real sense of having been to blame came to disturb her mind. That intense belief in herself which, as a rule, shielded her from uncomfortable feelings, deserted her now; she tried to argue herself into some more cheerful vein, but found it hopeless. Was it that she was weaker, and that her illness had shaken her nerves? When night fell and the household slept, memory came to confront her. Her selfishness filled her with remorse; how many things she could look back upon now, when Margaret, her sweetness, and her devotion never failing, had been counted as so little, tested by her own all-absorbing love of having her own way?

After all, how petty a thing she had urged her sacrifice for, and how easily the self-will that had in the end been obliged to give in might have done so before, and saved her!

A recognition, dim as yet, came to her of the beauty of her sister's character. How far apart they stood in feeling! How Margaret insisted on not only truth, but the highest expression of truth, as the only thing she cared for.

Tears chased each other down her face, and each morning found her pale and unrefreshed.

Want of sleep and the incessant torment of a newly awakened conscience made Grace unusually irritable, her gay spirits were fitful, and, indeed, were only used as a mask to hide the perpetual pain she had to bear, a pain so far, far, more agonizing than any bodily pain.

Mr. Sandford — who was, himself, out of

health — had no affection to enable him to support her provoking ways.

He was terribly annoyed and concerned about Margaret, he was upset and mortified by other things.

It was impossible for Mr. Drayton to have lost, as he had lost, without the fact being known far and wide, and Mr. Sandford's share was universally condemned. He was accused openly of having made a cat's-paw of the man whose genial laugh and careless ways had gained him the epithet of a " good fellow " from men who had neither suffered through him or known his counter-balancing want of attraction.

Mr. Sandford knew that had he not been a fool and a timid fool, just when he ought to have been bold, he would not have lost, but there was just that grain of truth in the accusation which made it sting.

The reputation of a man in business— who has not the root of honesty where honesty must be a *sine quâ non*—if respect is to be given; is like graceful species of fir-trees to be found on Scottish hills and in many a wood, where, instead of sending their roots well down into the earth, as do the other kinds, they spread close to the surface, and the first rough wind throws them over and exposes the shallow hold they have of mother earth. Mr. Sandford's name, once holding so high a place, began to be mentioned with a little reticence. A shake of the head or a shrug of the shoulders says a good deal, though it cannot be repeated. It has weight; gestures are often remembered when words, especially vague words, are forgotten.

Once a little beginning is made how easy is it to go on! People began again to remember that there was a great deal about poor Mr. Dorriman's affairs that had never been properly understood.

This feeling made itself felt. The first time Mr. Sandford wanted to carry through some measure with his usual heavy hand, the members of the Company, of which he was chairman, demurred. No one accused him openly, but there were certain things insinuated.

His quick sense of any failing towards himself made him instantly grasp the position of matters; and, though he mastered himself sufficiently to show no outward sign, he went home with rage in his heart, all the more terrible that it had had no outlet. It was at this inopportune time that Grace provoked him.

Mrs. Dorriman, in vain, tried to counsel the wilful girl, in private. She heard her unmoved. Day after day there were scenes, in which her provoking words stung him.

"Why should I not say what I think, my dear Mrs. Dorriman? I really cannot hold my tongue."

"I do not believe you are saying what you think. You speak on purpose to provoke my brother."

"And why should he not be provoked? Life gives me a great many trials. I should, myself, prefer another home; but if I am obliged to live here I am not going to speak or be silent according to Mr. Sandford's wishes, and I do not intend being a hypocrite."

"No one wishes you to be a hypocrite, but you need not say what you have to say disagreeably. You always make him angry, not so much by your words but by the way you speak the words."

"Mr. Sandford is a tyrant, and the more you give in to him the less you are likely to get. I hope I may never live to be as frightened and timid as you are!"

"I am not too timid to say what I think, if it is right to say it."

"Yes, you are! you look frightened, and that is enough for a man like your brother. Now I cannot really look frightened, because a man in a rage is to me a ridiculous object. It amuses me."

"I cannot help saying you have had one lesson! You once provoked my brother in such a way that you and Margaret went away, and poor Margaret has now to suffer; you might see that you do harm and not good;"

and Mrs. Dorriman felt so angry she did not measure her words. "You do not suffer, but she does, and but for you, but for your way of speaking to my brother, she would be safe with us, poor child!"

She had effectually stopped her for the moment, and, herself moved by this statement in words of thoughts often present to her, she rose and left the room.

She had said nothing that Grace had not remorsefully said to herself, but the very truth in her speech made her angry.

She heard Mr. Sandford's voice. He was calling his sister's name. He met her on the stairs in tears.

She passed him quickly, and indignant, and in a mood full of irritability, he strode into the drawing-room to Grace.

"I will have you know," he said in his angriest and loudest voice, "that I will not allow you to bully my sister."

"No," said Grace, languidly, "you like to monopolise that privilege!"

"How dare you speak to me in that way?"

"I dare speak in any way to you. Why are you to be always studied? and why is every one to treat you as though you were a being of another sphere? You do bully your sister, and you would bully me if I were to be in the very least afraid of you. But I am not. Your sister has been trying to make me see that you ought to be humoured—she drew an affecting picture and then wept over it."

He was white now, pale with rage.

"What do you know about my conduct to my sister? There is no one I more respect."

"Well, you have the oddest way of showing it I ever knew," and Grace made a provoking gesture of astonishment, and gave a laugh of derision.

This completely exhausted Mr. Sandford's very slight stock of patience. He went into a most fearful rage and said things that made Grace shiver. Pale in her turn she left the room, and for a second time left his house in anger.

She left without her things, wrapping herself up in her cloak, and resolved to go to her sister, and not to make a sign. She was quite, quite sure Mr. Drayton would receive her at any rate for a time, and she must make some new arrangement. Return here she never would.

Mrs. Dorriman heard the loud voice, and as soon as she had recovered her composure she hurried to the scene of action, to find Mr. Sandford ill, as he always was when passion got the mastery of him.

In her anxiety about him Grace was forgotten, and it was not till dinner-time that her departure was discovered, and poor Mrs. Dorriman felt as though troubles were indeed her portion.

Mr. Sandford did not rally as he usually did, and she on her own responsibility sent for the doctor.

He came and administered remedies. Then he told her privately that her brother had a serious complaint, and that agitation would one day be fatal to him.

"You must keep him quiet; he really must not be either worried or disturbed about anything," said the doctor, not unkindly, but anxious professionally, and determined to insist on his patient's having the only chance of living.

"If I can keep him quiet!" began poor Mrs. Dorriman, "but nothing I can do is of any use. Oh! indeed it is not my fault."

"Of course I do not mean to say it is," he answered hastily, "but I merely give you warning. This attack has been brought on by some violent emotion, and a repetition of it, *any* mental excitement, will put an end to his life."

Mrs. Dorriman went to his side when the doctor had gone, a whole world of remorse and pain in her heart.

She had been several months with him now, and, though she had never really forgotten the unspoken suspicion, it had been put into a remote corner of her memory. As she looked upon him and marked the careworn face and look of struggle his attack had left, she had a sense of having been treacherous towards him. What did it really matter? Supposing those papers contained some proof against him, would it be of any use confronting him with them?

She was conscious of two things—that the whole attitude of her mind had changed towards him, and that it had also altered towards her husband.

The various scenes she had gone through at Renton had had the effect of turning her thoughts gratefully towards the affection and the peace she had had with her husband.

She began to think of him more tenderly, and to see other possible conclusions than those she had arrived at.

This awakened tenderness, which could never comfort him now, made her feel as though, if she did read those papers, she would see nothing against her husband, and this conviction took a heavy load off her mind. Then came the other part of the problem—If her husband had been blameless what was her brother?

All the long years of neglect at school, all the harshness with which he had treated her in former years, seemed to have faded now, she had softened to him so much, and now as he slowly recovered she acknowledged this.

It was just when she had recognised him as her first duty now that the telegram imploring her, to go at once to Grace was put into her hand.

She was distressed beyond measure, but she could not do it, she could not agitate or annoy him now. She *could* not leave him.

It was indeed hard to her to send Jean from her but she had no confidence in other help, and she had the strongest feeling of a neglected duty if she now gave up helping the wayward girl.

Jean went unwilling. She had never been out of Scotland, and looked upon London as a sink of iniquity. She had some misgivings about her journey, and she went off with an idea fixed in her head that she was to be always upon her guard against plausible pickpockets, extortionate cabmen, and civilities which might mean robbery in the end.

She pinned Grace's address inside her dress, concealed her purse there, and was put into the train by Robert, who gave the guard charge of her, very much to her own indignation, " as though I was a little parcel," she said to herself.

She was in a second-class carriage and met with a few adventures; she was so "stand-off" to the two or three strangers who got in or out that they thought her a most disagreeable old woman, but Jean was only on her guard.

When they changed carriages and Jean was once more seated, a young woman passed and re-passed and finally got into the carriage and sat down opposite to her. She was very fair and had a lovely pink colour in her cheeks. She fidgeted a good deal, got up and shook her dress, and finally said, in accents of dismay,

"Oh, what shall I do? I have lost my ticket and I have no money with me!"

Jean, who was alone in the carriage, eyed her attentively but spoke not a word.

The young woman began to cry.

"Help me!" she said; "help me! I am alone and friendless!"

Jean still said nothing; she noticed that as they stopped at a station her sobs subsided and that she drew back into a corner and avoided observation. This roused her suspicions, and, when they started again, the person, hitherto in such despair, began to grow not a little impertinent.

"I wonder if people pay by weight in this train?" she said, airily, determined to unlock the silent lips of the stout and much wrapped-up figure in front of her.

This taunt about her size did rouse Jean.

"If you've *paid* for your ticket you probably know," she said, in her best English, and extremely indignant.

This answer completely extinguished all

wish for conversation on the part of her opposite neighbour, but she still fidgeted about, trying first one seat and then another, and, sitting down beside Jean, she fumbled about and pressed against her, altogether making herself most objectionable.

The journey came to an end; the ticket-collector came to the door and Jean put her hand in her pocket—her purse was safe, luckily, in the front of her dress—the ticket was gone! Greatly to her surprise the young woman immediately produced one.

Jean hunted in vain, her ticket was nowhere to be found, and her dismay was great. She had a confused notion that she was in some way breaking the law, and, though outwardly she kept calm, she was in a most fearful state really, and she did not know what to do.

The guard fortunately came up to see what the stoppage was, and was accompanied by a policeman.

"What was the matter?" he asked.

Before Jean could answer, the policeman stretched out his hand and touched the young woman, who had been vainly trying to get out. She turned pale—through what Jean now saw was paint.

"You are wanted," and, turning to Jean, he said, "has she taken anything of yours, ma'am?"

Looking at the ticket the guard laughed and answered,

"She has taken your ticket, old lady. '*From Renton to London.*' She only got in an hour ago."

Poor Jean! all her life long she will believe in policemen from henceforward. Indeed, when she went from St. Pancras to the station for Wandsworth she refused to pay her cab till the policeman standing near told her what the fare was, amusing the bystanders not a little by her determined attitude and the suspicious look she gave the cabman.

When she reached Grace, her fatigue, her adventures, everything gave way to compassion. For Grace was very ill, and needed good nursing and care, and, to poor Jean's eyes, the lodging and all belonging to it was not fit for any Christian, certainly not for a Scotchwoman.

She wondered a good deal that Margaret never came near her sister, and made up her mind to go and look her up: Mrs. Dorriman had charged her to be a mother to both bairns, and she fully intended keeping her promise.

In the meantime Margaret's little poem had been published, and she had received three golden sovereigns for her work. She knew so little of the value of literary work that she was not in the very least surprised; she felt only the deepest thankfulness that, if she had a gift, she could turn it to account for her beloved sister.

Her poem was very touching, full of the faults of one whose education had never been extensive, but when she saw it in print she noticed a few alterations she considered improvements, and took for granted that these alterations were made as a matter of course by the editor. This was evidently the use of having an editor. Then she began calculating how many of these poems she could write in a week. Say she wrote four. Why there was at once twelve guineas a week; a livelihood, a large income! Why, oh why, had she not thought of this before?

The impressions of her mind flowed naturally into rhyme. There was great beauty of thought, though much sameness in its delivery on paper. Her reading with Mrs. Dorriman had not been thrown away, and she began to be able to concentrate her thoughts on her work. The happiness of her life which she had missed, set all to a minor key, but it made her poems more beautiful. To touch the feelings of others, to appeal to their hearts, there must be reality, and reality only can exist from personal experience.

Sometimes the extraordinary dreariness of her life appalled her. To rise day after day, knowing that a secret dread of a possible tragedy, enacted in her house, pursued her; to see no one, to go nowhere, since she was not allowed to cross the threshold. She had no idea that these facts, told to any one, would have immediately brought her release, and that any one, knowing what her life was, would have formed a juster conclusion of the state her husband was in.

But the fear of having to leave, and to be parted from her child, made all else nothing to her, and when she met her husband, he hardly spoke to her. She never saw him without his servant being present, and she could not bear appealing to her husband before him. She could not bear discussing her sister's illness in his hearing.

Every possible opportunity she tried to get that key of the front door, or permission to go out, but each time was met by peals of laughter, of *senseless* laughter, and refusal.

Her husband's last idea was the most frantic jealousy of the doctor, who had been a little won over by Mrs. Drayton's youth and grace and charm of manner.

Before him Mr. Drayton was always perfectly quiet, and even well-bred, a little sullen, which was, the doctor thought, natural since he must resent the deprivation of any stimulants; but he was satisfied from his observations that he was really kept from them, and saw nothing to point suspicion in another direction.

He regretted never seeing the young wife now, and expressed his regret to Mr. Drayton.

He was surprised to see an angry flush rise in his face, but concluded that perhaps there had been some conjugal difference, and that she did not choose to appear.

When Margaret first contrived to send her little poem to good Mr. Skidd, the editor of the "Industrious Workman," she had done it through her nurse, who had grown warmly attached to her mistress. She was quite young—this was her first place, and she came to the conclusion that if this was the life led by rich people, the poor had many more pleasures.

Margaret read her poem to her, which she but vaguely took in, and she also read her the note she wrote to the editor.

She had no knowledge of him except that at first the doctor had told her she could get books there, when she had asked him, he had also spoken highly of him as a cultivated and intellectual man, who had done a great deal towards spreading wholesome cheap literature, and that he edited a weekly paper of much merit.

Her idea, now, was to write something longer and more important. She had two great incentives to write: she had that something to say, without which all writing falls so flat; and she wished to get money for her sister.

Mr. Skidd received her proposal to write a book of poetry with some amusement.

The unknown gentleman who brought out her little poems at his own expense, after they had appeared in the paper, and who received for her the few shillings Mr. Skidd considered them worth, might not stretch his generosity so far as to embark in a larger book—but he would see. He spoke, therefore, rather vaguely to the young woman who came as messenger, so vaguely that Margaret imagined she *must* try, in some way, and have an interview with the man herself.

But how to accomplish this? True, there was a back door, but she could not bear going out through the connivance of the servant, who was cook and who was a disagreeable woman at all times. Fortune favoured her, however, in a few days. She was walking in the garden one afternoon with her nurse and baby when some one came to the front door with a message, which caused the grumpy man-servant to go into the house for a few seconds. Quick as thought, Margaret slipped out of her prison, and hurried along the road.

She was dizzy with excitement and the

sense of freedom — to see Grace — and to arrange about her book.

Her face was glowing as she moved along. She must first see Grace, and then hurry on to do her business.

When she reached Grace's lodgings she was met by a home-like, kindly face; and Jean, forgetting everything but that she had a hard life of it, took her to her arms as though she had been a bairn of her own.

Margaret's tears were never very near the surface, but she had lived a life so unnatural and so repressed, she had been so entirely without kindness or sympathy for so long, that she broke down now, and sobbed upon good, honest, Jean's broad shoulder, sensible only of the sweetness and comfort of the relief.

"My poor bairn, my poor bairn!" Jean kept on saying, and then, recollecting that she ought not to allow her to give way, she said, "but you'll no be fit to see Miss Grace, and you just a blurred objick," and this reflection also stopped Margaret's tears and caused her to lift up her head and try to compose herself.

"How is my sister? How is Grace, dear Jean?"

"She's no just fit to dance the houlachan," said Jean, gaily, who had her own private way of pronouncing most words, "but she's not that bad. Eh, my dear, come and see her; she's been wearying for you, sair, sair."

Margaret went upstairs, and in another moment the sisters were once more together.

Grace was lying on the sofa, and Margaret found her looking better than she expected. She was a softened edition of the old Grace, still fitful, capricious, but full of tenderness for her sister, whose life she had so completely spoiled.

"Why, darling, have you never been here before?" she asked; "I have sent you so many notes and have had such scanty answers. You never tell me of yourself; you never tell me what I want to know."

"I have so little to say of myself. My husband has been ill, and, since his illness, he cannot bear my going out, and I came to-day because I could slip away."

"But tell me one thing, darling, only one. Why stay with him? Why not leave him?"

"Because of baby; I cannot desert my little one, Grace: and if I left him merely because he is unkind and allows me no liberty and is 'odd,' he would have the right to keep baby, not I, its mother."

"Then if that is the law it is abominable!" exclaimed Grace.

"I think it *is* terrible," said Margaret; "even if he was cruel, if he struck me, if he were in other ways infamous, I might leave him; I should be free; but even then it is doubtful if I might have my child."

"And we boast of English justice!" exclaimed Grace.

"It is cruelly unjust," said Margaret. "Oh darling, how often we have laughed at women wanting their 'rights,' and made fun of those who made a stir about having votes: but this one thing, this one frightful injustice, makes me feel that women should, in some way, be able to make their great needs felt; surely a mother should have equal rights with the father, and have something to say in a child's destiny!"

"And we have to submit, and I, *I* have brought you into this position!" and Grace burst into tears.

Jean hurried into the room.

"Bairns, my dear bairns, whist, for any sake. You'll make me feel I did wrong in leaving the two of you together."

"We were talking of an unjust law," said Margaret; "we were talking of my child, Jean, and that *if* I ever left my husband, he would have it probably, and not me."

"It's a man made that law," said Jean, "and it's a real cruel one and not Christian. I never had any opinion of men, they're just poor creatures all round, poor selfish creatures —except, maybe, the police," she added, with a sense of ingratitude for the way in which a policeman had helped her in her hour of need.

"Tell me of your baby, Margaret," said Grace, turning with real interest to her sister; "it is more than a year old now, is it not?"

"My little darling is a year and almost three months old, in five days now it will be fifteen months old. It can run about, and calls me so prettily. Oh, darling, I wish, I wish it were with me at this moment. I feel so anxious if I am away from it; only once before, since its birth, have I been away."

"And does that man shut you up, darling? Do you mean to say that those smoky trees and that walled-in place, looking like a prison, is all you have? Oh, your life is one long trial!"

Margaret did not speak; her life was so utterly wretched, so utterly devoid of hope, that she could not speak of it.

"I have baby," she said, softly, "and, Gracie, dearest, when one is very wretched God is very near."

The sisters parted with all the anguish of a vagueness about their next meeting, which filled them both with a sense of having nothing to look forward to, and Margaret tore herself away and hurried into Mr. Skidd's presence.

Mrs. Dorriman had boldly authorised Jean to look to Mr. Sandford for all expenses, so that she no longer cared about the money so much.

But this lessened sense of requirement did not in any way make her gratitude to the editor for his kindness, less. With no real knowledge to guide her she did not know that everything must bear the test of criticism, and that it would have been false kindness to encourage her to write without any merit in sight.

But Mr. Skidd had discovered real merit in all Margaret did; there was the impress of truth, and no fictitious feeling. The cry was the cry of a starved, human soul pining for sympathy and an outlet, under a life of great misery and repression, haunted by a never-ending fear.

He was so amazed when Margaret stood before him—at her youth and the graceful way she expressed her thanks, that he was dumb before her.

Next a vivid colour blushed over his bald head, for he remembered that he stood in his shirt-sleeves.

He was too honest a man to accept her thanks for more than he had done, and he puzzled her considerably by his allusion to the great appreciation of a gentleman from London.

"But you published my little poem," she asked, not a little perplexed by his statements.

"Certainly, madam! In the first instance I did, but this gentleman, a literary gentleman, happened to call the very day I was reading your first poem, and he liked it, and he brought it out afterwards and took charge of the trifle I sent you for it; I hope that was all right and that you received it. I hold his receipt, and I imagined he was authorised by you."

"Oh, thank you! Yes. I got the money all right," said Margaret, much bewildered, and wondering who this could have been.

She found also that Mr. Skidd could not promise anything about her poem in an enlarged form till he had seen it, and had time to consult this mysterious friend, who by his account appreciated her short poems so much.

It was delightful to think she might have a larger audience and command a public who might be equally appreciative. Mr. Skidd began to discuss her poetry with her, and he gave her many useful hints.

"The fault of your poetry, madam, is that it wants variety. People get tired of perpetual sorrow and all that sort of thing. You write very prettily. Give us something cheerful, make the birds twitter and the sun shine, cultivate brightness, people do not like always being in mourning."

"But if I am not happy I cannot write what I do not feel," objected Margaret.

"Oh, yes you can; you get the trick of the thing and you will easily do it."

Margaret knew this to be impossible, but before she had time to repeat her negative a well-remembered face came before her, and Sir Albert Gerald, filled with happiness at meeting her so unexpectedly, came up with an outstretched hand. Mr. Skidd was immensely annoyed.

"And you make believe not to know who buys your poem," he exclaimed; "I call that humbug—and you," he said sharply, turning to Sir Albert, "why could you not be open about it?"

"But did *you* buy my poems? Are you the literary man from whose appreciation I have received so much encouragement," and Margaret, mortified and disappointed, turned to go away.

At any rate *she* knew nothing, and Mr.

Skidd was ashamed of the momentary suspicion that had filled him.

"No, this lady was acting on the square; as for the man . . . . . "

The little man felt as he looked at them that a whole drama was being played out before his eyes, the air was full of some secret thing in connection with these two.

Sir Albert, deferential and respectful, was evidently quite absorbed in the tall, graceful figure before him, who stood cold and apparently determined to show no satisfaction in his presence.

Mr. Skidd was a good judge of character.

"I'll be bound there is no harm in *her*," he said, and so saying left them to themselves.

CHAPTER VIII.

"You believe, do you not, that my being here is an accident?" Sir Albert said courteously. "I have been interested in your writing, and I am glad it has found appreciation."

She raised her head and spoke to him hurriedly, "You are kind—you mean to be kind—but you have no idea what a bitter, bitter blow this is to me—and what a terrible disappointment!"

"You misunderstand the whole thing," he said, moved almost beyond his powers of control when he noted how her bloom had faded, and how terrible the traces of anxiety in her face showed what her life was. "It is true that I have managed the publication for you, but I assure you that your poems have met with the highest praise, and that, though I did bring them out for you (it seems such a little thing to do for you), I have just now received a letter from the editor of one of the highest class of magazines to show you. Your name is unknown to him—he merely treats your poems as coming from a stranger—you are a complete stranger to him. Will you read it?"

He held it towards her. While finding fault with one or two lines, objecting to a word here and there, he acknowledged in warm terms the beauty of imagery, the flow of thought, the purity of the lines sent him, and considered it indicated unusual power, and that the author should be encouraged to try a longer flight.

Poor Margaret! The present and all the trials of her life were forgotten; the sweetness of this praise coming at a moment when her heart was starved, and all her brilliant and glowing imagination was pent up within the dreary walls of her most unhappy home, was almost overpowering. She held both hands out to the man who had proved himself so real a friend—her colour flushed into her cheek, and tears of gratitude sparkled in her eyes.

It was the sorest trial to poor Sir Albert not to be able to tell her that he could not bear gratitude from her. He stood gazing at her, as one spell-bound, clasping her hands till she withdrew them, with a struggle going on in his heart that was almost beyond him.

Then she turned to go, and her last words were at once a pang and a reward.

"I will always trust you," she said, earnestly, "you will be my critic and my judge; if I write nonsense you will be a real friend and say so. I feel so grateful to you! From henceforward I shall feel I have indeed a brother."

He muttered something, feeling miserable, and frightened of her seeing it, and he watched her go, knowing that his life was only cheered by the hope of befriending her—thankful that she had this one great gift to save her from despair, and yet fully aware that, as far as he was concerned, her utter unconsciousness of his continued love was an additional pain to him.

Then he went into one or two business details with Mr. Skidd; delighted that little man by corroborating his high opinion of the little poems by showing him the letter he had—and went to London, depressed and unhappy. He had gained nothing by this accidental interview except the conviction that she had so entirely forgotten his love that she proffered the brotherly tie as entirely satisfactory to him, as to her. And yet, in his heart of hearts, he knew that this attitude towards him was the only possible one for such as her if she allowed him to help her and to be her friend.

Mrs. Dorriman, missing Jean at every turn, was in a measure consoled by the gruff kindness of her brother to her.

She was so accustomed to his manner that she felt the kindness and did not resent his roughness.

She was happier since she had seen Jean, whose letter, faithfully detailing her adventures, was very amusing. But she asked herself what was to be the end of it all?

Grace, who must have some settled home, and poor Margaret, who seemed to be so completely a prisoner, and not able to go and look after her sister, were both perplexing problems.

But as life goes on we learn not to trouble so much about things, we feel that a Hand does guide and guard us, and bring all things right—and Mrs. Dorriman, looking back upon her life, was every day learning this deeper lesson.

She was surprised now to receive a good many visits, a thing she had hitherto been unaccustomed to, at Renton Place.

The few neighbours around, living within easy distance, had hardly realised that Mrs.

Dorriman had come to Renton to live there. When she first went to Renton, with all the kindness of heart of the neighbours, and a real wish to make acquaintance with a person of whom all the world spoke well, there was a pardonable amount of curiosity among some.

A man reputed to be a millionnaire, and who had a romantic attachment for his first wife, might also make a good husband to a second wife. Then also the question of the girls who were to have lived with him and who did not live with him. Margaret's marriage to a man "old enough to be her grandfather," and a certain little mystery of where it had all been made up, gave that interest in the doings at Renton Place which blossomed into activity in the shape of visits.

The first person who felt a visit due from her was Mrs. Wymans, who had the excuse of an apology to make for having handled the domestic affairs of Mr Sandford, with a certain freedom, before Mrs. Dorriman.

Most people would have thought that the

apology might have been made before, or might be left alone now; but this conditional tense in which her friends put the case was met by Mrs. Wymans with plausible reasons. Certainly she had always thought of going—but till now—did any one know that Mrs. Dorriman was anything more than a visitor? Had she known that she was really to be resident . . . . Why of course it would be very rude not to call.

Mrs. Dorriman was not at all inclined to despise the proffered olive-branch. She had no distaste for acquaintances, and was so evidently glad to see that people intended to be kind to her, that the infection spread. From being liked she became extremely popular; a person never sure enough of her facts to contradict anybody is always approved of; and after being spoken of as poor Mrs. Dorriman for many months she was now talked of as dear Mrs. Dorriman, being one of those women who, for some inexplicable reason, is never mentioned without an adjective.

The visits were made and returned—the only drawback being that Mr. Sandford had never yet been seen by any one—though Mrs. Wymans, who always posed as having done or seen a little more than her neighbours, avowed to having seen the back of his head upon one occasion, which, if true, certainly proved that he was capable of being in two places at once.

Truth to tell, the *rapprochement* between the brother and sister was not productive of entire satisfaction to Mr. Sandford.

If Mrs. Dorriman's conscience was so sensitive that she felt like a traitor towards her brother, because of certain papers she knew of, the contents of which might *possibly* betray something against him, his conscience, though not sensitive, had a far far heavier weight upon it, though it did not press upon him continually.

It was impossible to live with a woman

so meek, so gentle, and so unselfish, without learning to like her, but the liking produced much acute uneasiness; and at times his rough manner was more a mask for his uncomfortable feelings than for any other reason.

He was up and out again, though he felt that he had not quite his old clearness of perception, he was more easily tired and he was always thankful to get home.

That home was indeed changed to him now. The cheerfulness and serenity, the evenness of Mrs. Dorriman's temper made him look forward to going home, where his most trifling wishes were attended to, and when he had that *certainty* of being met in the same quiet way, of having no fluctuations in manner, which gives the real home feeling.

Mrs. Dorriman was not perfect, she was a woman who possessed no great gifts, and she was constitutionally timid, and not much fitted to form an opinion about subjects outside those of domestic interest; but she did understand that a man, tired and worried by affairs outside his home, required rest and refreshment in it, and she knew how to give both.

The dreariness that had once obtained had long vanished. All inside the house was light and bright and cheerful for him now, and each day sent him home with this recognition deeper in his heart, and more remorseful because of certain acts of his which now never could be undone.

Mrs. Wymans, when she made her appearance at Renton, had rehearsed her apology, and then found that it must be put differently.

The extreme quiet of Mrs. Dorriman's manner was a check she had hardly counted upon. When they had that encounter in the railway carriage the poor little lady had been troubled and nervous, her manner was agitated; and Mrs. Wymans, who was a shrewd observer, saw that she stopped the conversation about her brother from a sense of right, and that she was evidently not resenting it in a sisterly fashion.

From this she drew several inferences, every one of which had to be laid aside now.

"Your brother, I hear, has been so ill we did not like to intrude, and before—you went away ——" she said, which was not in the least what she had meant to say.

"Yes," said Mrs. Dorriman, "we went away, and had you been so kind as to call before this I could not have seen you, my brother has been so very ill."

"And you have no nurse?" said Mrs. Wymans, betraying her knowledge of the internal economy of the household. "You must find the nursing very troublesome and most fatiguing. I know of an excellent woman who could come at a moment's notice."

"Thank you, but I am happy to say that the fatigue, like the illness, lies in the past. My brother is quite well again, and out and about his usual business."

"Of course he likes his business, he is so successful; the trial is where hard work is not successful," and Mrs. Wymans spoke feelingly.

"I think my brother meets with some success and probably some trials also, but these are only words too; we never talk of business together, and I know nothing about his."

"Really! Forgive me, dear Mrs. Dorriman, but then where is the sympathy? And a woman has such sharp eyes. I never rest till I know every single thing that is going on—that is my way of showing sympathy."

"But it must tire your husband, does it not? A woman can see only one side, and then she cannot help in the way of advice. Her advice cannot be useful."

"That is only a notion of yours," said Mrs. Wymans, a little nettled, "and why should a woman only know one side of a thing?"

"Because she only hears her husband's views; of course his private affairs cannot be talked over with another person, therefore the wife's views must be a little one-sided."

"Oh no, mine are not. I hear a thing and see a great many sides all at once."

"Perhaps you are cleverer than I am," said Mrs. Dorriman, in all humility, glad that at any rate the question of the Rivers girls had not cropped up.

Mrs. Wymans eyed her keenly, anxious to make out whether she was speaking satirically or not. Somewhat reassured on that point by Mrs. Dorriman's placid face, she drew a little nearer her and said confidentally,

"What a sad thing Mrs. Drayton's position is!"

"In what way?" Mrs. Dorriman received a dreadful shock by this sudden touch upon the subject.

"Why, her husband being poor instead of rich, and some other things."

"Do you mind telling me what other things?" and Mrs. Dorriman was alarmed as well as annoyed.

"Why, if you do not know of any thing, . . . but if it is not true, I had better not repeat it."

"You really must tell me what you mean," and Mrs. Dorriman, the gentlest of women, had so to speak all her feathers ruffled now.

"People say he drinks," answered Mrs.

Wymans, with that sudden misgiving as to the wisdom of her words which made her wish them unsaid immediately they had passed her lips.

"That I am sure is not the case," returned Mrs. Dorriman; she felt quite convinced that had there been any truth about this she would have heard it counted against him when her brother had been so incensed with her and had said many bitter things.

"I am so very glad to hear it," and Mrs. Wymans lost her sense of discomfort, since it was not true.

"It was a curious marriage for a young girl to make," she remarked abruptly, since she found Mrs. Dorriman's silence a little oppressive.

"I think it was; but, though my brother offered them a home, he had, of course, no real authority over them."

"Ah," said Mrs. Wymans, enchanted to have got at the root of the matter, "people were rather puzzled at his having taken them up so much; do you very much mind telling me, dear Mrs. Dorriman, how it all was? What was the real bond of union?"

"Why should I mind telling you so simple a thing?" and Mrs. Dorriman's amused face was quite a little shock to her visitor; "they are his wife's nieces: he is their uncle by marriage, and being, as you are probably aware, devoted to his wife's memory, he was glad to befriend them."

"And is this really all?" exclaimed Mrs. Wymans, who could hardly get over her disappointment. "Why we all thought—every one thought—and people said something else."

"People are wrong," said Mrs. Dorriman, with a laugh that was a very genuine one; "I cannot myself understand the interest taken in these private matters, but that is the simple fact. Mr. Rivers and my brother married two sisters, who were devoted to each other. When Mrs. Rivers died she recommended her children to Mrs. Sandford, and at her death my brother promised to befriend them. It seems to me such a simple thing."

"It certainly does," and Mrs. Wymans rose to go, and bid farewell to Mrs. Dorriman, who was conscious only of one terrible speech; was it true that Mr. Drayton did —— that —— and, if it was true, were they right in taking all for granted and leaving Margaret at his mercy? But for the doctor's prohibition she would have gone straight to her brother and laid her new anxieties before him. But she remembered that he was not to be agitated or excited, and she resolutely sat still till all her own excited thoughts became calmer. She took up her knitting and worked on mechanically, while this new responsibility made her feel as though nothing in the world, of such moment, had ever come before her. It was an evil unknown to her; in the old days her father was a man both abstemious and refined in his surroundings, and since her marriage, though she saw terrible accounts in the papers, she had lived so little in any town, and had seen so little that was evil, that she considered people made almost unnecessary fuss about tectotalism; she could not imagine such a fearful thing as drinking touching her order, though she knew it obtained among some poor miserable creatures, of whom she seldom thought without a shudder of sorrow, mingled with disgust.

To think of Margaret, with all her great love of purity and peace, exposed to so horrible a thing, was something absolutely terrible to her; so perfectly appalling that she started up, feeling as though every moment was a cruel wrong to the girl she had learned to love so dearly. She went to her brother's room; he was sitting up, and she sat down beside him in a flutter of spirits that made her incoherent.

"You have had a visitor," he began, with a laugh in which there was not much mirth.

"Only Mrs. Wymans," she answered, with indifference.

"If she could hear you! She is a person of great consequence in her own estimation."

"I wonder why she called," his sister said,

absently, doubtful as to her capability of putting the question without causing any excitement.

"I'll tell you," he answered; "there is a great deal of curiosity about Drayton just now; before this attack of mine I was driven wild by all manner of questions about him. He is a great fool to make a mystery of his address; there is no reason he should do so; he answers no letters, he leaves every one to conjecture things, and in this beautiful world if a thing is not fully understood, the worst interpretation and not the best is the accepted one."

"Then you think there is no reason for his shutting himself up?"

"There can be no reason. Margaret is not likely to give him cause for jealousy, and the man is in the possession of all his senses."

"Always, and at all times?" and Mrs. Dorriman leaned forward, breathing quickly and watching his face very anxiously.

"Anne," said Mr. Sandford, and this name

from him was an especial sign of kindness towards her, "has any one told you anything? Depend upon it it is only gossip."

"It may be gossip, I trust it may be untrue; but why is Margaret, so to speak, shut up? She cannot go out even for a walk beyond the grounds; Jean says she has not been to see Grace for ever so long, and there must be some reason for his never answering any letter."

"I never heard this before. What do you mean about Margaret? I think you are speaking great nonsense."

"Jean says that the poor thing never gets out. At first she went out and he went with her—followed her like a shadow—now he does not go himself, and she is kept a perfect prisoner. No one is allowed to go near the house. I assure you, brother, I have been longing for you to be well to speak about it."

"The man must be mad," exclaimed Mr. Sandford, and then he noticed his sister's face.

"You have heard something, you have something more to say?" and his own face flushed.

"Brother, do not excite yourself. You know the doctor is afraid of your being ill if you do."

"Well, then, don't make mysteries," he said very angrily, and with much of his old violence.

"I am sure," said the poor woman, hurt at such an accusation, "I do not wish to make mysteries, but Mrs. Wymans told me that she had heard he drank. Now, I am not quite sure if she put it quite that way or if she asked me if he drank."

"Not a bit of it. If he does, it is something quite new. He was a very abstemious man. You might recollect his headaches, and saying wine increased those headaches."

"So I do," exclaimed Mrs. Dorriman, joyfully; "how tiresome it is that I forgot this when that woman was here. She spoke so meaningly," and Mrs. Dorriman as usual considered herself somehow altogether to blame.

Mr. Sandford said no more, but he lay back, thinking. He blamed himself, justly, for having been the person to bring this man to the house for his own end—and now . . .

He was free of further blame; he had heard rumours in connection with Mr. Drayton's family that had greatly disturbed him, and *then* he had done his best to prevent his marrying Margaret; his conscience had plenty to bear but not this—only he might have spoken more plainly, he might have told her or his sister something that had come to his knowledge. Then, when too late, he *knew*.

He was better, but his strength was not coming back quickly, and business matters, the position he had held, everything connected with the past, began to shrink in importance.

But Margaret! Something must be done at once about her; a terrible dread came to him about her.

"One thing you must do at once," he said, aloud, following out his own thoughts, "you must write to Jean without delay; enclose her a cheque, and tell her it is important that she should give it, and letters from you, to Margaret, into her own hand. Write to Margaret and tell her she is to let you know the truth, and what her position is—write *at once*," he repeated, as though his sister, who was thoroughly alarmed, needed any second telling.

Jean was, on the whole, easier about Grace, who had made a surprising rally. She was able to be up and enjoy her meals; she was also able to enjoy the visits of no less a person than Paul Lyons.

Margaret being married and out of his reach, that young man had conceived a great affection for her sister, now a very softened and subdued likeness of herself at Lornbay.

"You are not Margaret, but you remind me of her," he said sentimentally.

"We are sisters. I think there is a likeness."

Grace was extremely amused by his sentiment and by the little speeches he made her.

She had always rather liked him, and was always tolerant of the little ways that had so provoked her high-minded sister.

"I am not sure about it, personally," he said, "I meant your voice and your manner, and something altogether."

"We have the same kind of nose," laughed Grace. "Never mind, Mr. Lyons, I like you to be loyal to my sister; I never, *never*, could come up to her, and I know it!"

"You—you are more like than you were last year. Sometimes I think you *very* like Margaret," said Mr. Lyons, consolingly.

"Thank you. I know that is a very high compliment from you."

"Don't you think, Miss Rivers, that Margaret *might*, she might, have been happier with a fellow like me than with an old madman like Drayton?—that's what hurts me so much," said the young man.

"Of course she would have been happier, but everything went wrong," and Grace blushed vividly. "I sent everything wrong, and, poor, poor darling, she sacrificed herself to save me. Oh, Mr. Lyons! you never can say anything bad enough for me to feel it unjust. I hate myself more and more every day," and, much to his consternation, Grace, usually mocking at tears, shed them now.

"I declare you are so like Margaret that I am getting to be very fond of you," exclaimed Paul, "please don't cry, it makes me feel so .... funny!" and he looked unhappy, also.

"Oh, if I could *do* anything!" exclaimed poor Grace, who was, now she was stronger, less able to remain passive, and who was utterly and entirely miserable about her sister.

"If one could only shoot the fellow!" said Paul, vindictively.

"You see even if I could go out that wretched man keeps guard; he will not let Jean see my poor Margaret. A little while ago there was a back door, now that is shut up."

"But why does she not walk out of the house?"

"Because of her baby. She will not leave it and he will not allow her to take it with her, and I do not quite understand about the law, but, even if she took it, they might force her to send it back to him, so she says."

"Grace," said young Lyons, and he looked as though he had quite made up his mind to something, "I wish you would marry me. I am quite in earnest," he said, getting very red at her expression of amazement; "you see, if I was *her* brother I might be of some use."

Perhaps never was a proposal made so oddly, and never one so open to offence taken in such good part.

"No, Mr. Lyons," said Grace, laughing, while tears stood in her eyes; "you are a dear, kind-hearted boy; do you suppose I would consent to anything of the kind? Put all nonsense out of your head and try to see if there is anything in the world we can do. You are more able, you are stronger than I am; think!"

Paul Lyons thought, but he could see no way of helping Margaret unless she would help herself.

They neither of them knew what had only lately happened at the Limes. When Margaret, her heart full of gratitude about her writing, a glow of deep and checquered feeling making her steps lighter, as she went homewards, had been kept at the door waiting a weary while.

When at length the servant came Mr. Drayton was with him, and he had been so excited and so violent that the man could hardly control him.

"I am sure, ma'am, he is mad," he said to the terrified girl, "and I will see and get the doctor to-morrow; I cannot well leave him just now."

"Oh, pray, do not leave him!" said Margaret, terrified; "but to-morrow, yes, something must be done to-morrow."

She had made up her mind, as she stood trembling before him, that she would go, and she would take her child; surely, if he was mad—and she knew he must be mad—no one would take her child from her.

Next day, so soon as baby was awake, she roused the nurse. She had great difficulty in telling her what she meant to do; she meant to go now at once, while, as she thought, her husband slept, and the nurse might follow later.

"He will not wish to detain you," she said, "once we are safe away."

"But who will pay my wages?" asked the nurse, who did not at all see why she should risk her earnings or be left in the house with a madman when her charge and her mistress were gone.

"Of course that will be all right," said Margaret, with dignity.

"Are you sure, ma'am? because they say here you had no money, that your sister is living in a very poor way, and that you married master for his money."

Margaret's face was one flame.

"You are quite forgetting yourself," she said, and then the sting of these words made her turn away. Here was a truth—she had acknowledged to herself—put in the coarsest possible way to her! Had she a right to resent it?

She dressed her baby and herself, put up a few necessaries, and then knelt down and asked for help and guidance. It could not be wrong to go, for she was sure that her husband was mad; she must go and she must take her baby, who was hers; she was sure if she stayed that her husband would do her an injury; she had long had a vague fear, but last night had made her tremble; supposing he broke out in this way when the man was not by his side! She was trembling now as she went downstairs.

"Baby must keep quiet," she whispered; but how could baby know? As they passed her husband's door her frightened and close embrace alarmed and hurt the child, and she set up a tremendous roar. Margaret went to the front door; no key was there; she turned to the drawer to look and found her husband beside her.

"Where are you going?" he thundered, holding her shoulder as in a vice.

"I am going out," she answered, trying to speak, quivering with fear all the time.

"You do not go out at that door! and besides how can you go out with your precious child in the rain?"

Poor Margaret looked up and there indeed she saw that it was raining heavily.

Her heart sank and she paused irresolute.

At that moment the key turned in the lock, and the man came in.

"I have been to the doctor and he is coming directly," he said, and with a feeling of being baffled, though only for the time, poor Margaret turned her weary steps upstairs.

She was over-excited, and cried with the passion that comes from weakness, as from despair.

Then she left her child upstairs, and prepared to see the doctor. Through him she would surely be able to arrange something.

No one, she kept saying to herself, would wish her to stay with a madman, no one could leave a child in his keeping.

And she went to the sitting-room, and when she heard the doctor come she fled swiftly towards him, and took him upstairs to her own room. She would lay everything before him, and he would help her.

And he, looking at her flushed face and great excitement of manner, wondered whether she was going to tell him about some illness of her own ; and conscious of a certain prejudice against her, because of her marriage to this man, and a farewell he had witnessed between her and—Sir Albert Gerald.

CHAPTER IX.

Since that first interview Dr. Jones had had with the poor wife his feelings of admiration and pity had changed a good deal.

The explanation of her position lowered her considerably in his eyes. Perhaps no one sees the utter emptiness of life, and the non-importance of wealth, more than a medical man, who sees how little happiness it brings to any one; how little (standing by itself) it does for poor humanity.

He was disgusted when he saw that there was apparently no excuse for her; and he was shocked when he saw a farewell between her and a young man as he passed Mr. Skidd's shop, because here was evidently a lover. Her face he could not see, but Sir Albert's expression was unmistakeable.

Margaret, having no clue to his coldness and evident disapproval, felt speaking difficult, far more difficult than she had thought.

"I want to speak to you," she said, colouring under his searching gaze. "I want to tell you about my husband. I am very miserable, and I am very much frightened."

"Humph!" said Dr. Jones, "let us leave the misery upon one side, and talk about your fears; what makes you afraid?"

"My husband's violence. He was so very violent yesterday and this morning; I am afraid of his doing me an injury—I am afraid because of my child," and Margaret shivered.

"What made him violent?"

"He cannot bear my going out. He never allows me to go out, I am a prisoner here!"

He remembered having seen her out, and in his heart believed she was deliberately telling him a lie.

"What do you want to go out for?" he asked, roughly. "What do you mean by 'going out'?"

"I want to see my sister oftener."

Another lie he thought. "Why don't you brave him and go?" he said, trying her; "you might leave him altogether."

"Because I am told that if I leave he can keep my child!" said Margaret, passionately.

"Of course he can."

"It seems so hard," she said.

"Does it? I do not agree with you; why should a man be deprived of his child any more than a woman?"

"But if a man—is—mad?" whispered poor Margaret.

"Oh, that's where you are, is it! Well, I do not think that word is applicable here. There is temper, and there *was* drink. You will forgive my saying that, as you married Mr. Drayton, you took him for better or for worse. I do not think his health is good, and his temper is—well, irritable—that is the worst."

"Then you cannot help me!" and poor Margaret, who had hoped much from him, felt cruelly disappointed.

"How can I help you?" he asked, impatiently. "You wish me, *for some reason of your own,* to say that your husband is mad— which I have seen nothing to prove—and I will *not* say what I do not believe."

"I do not wish you to say it; I wish nothing but what is true and right: but I cannot understand how you, a medical man and experienced, can think Mr. Drayton quite right," pleaded Margaret; "if you could only see him as I have seen him!" and she stopped, afraid of betraying emotion to one so evidently lacking in sympathy.

"Of course, if I saw him with your eyes," began the doctor, coldly, all the more upon his guard because he was conscious that in spite of disapproval, in spite of what he knew and what he had seen, he was beginning to be influenced by her passionate appeal to him.

"We need not discuss this matter any longer," said Margaret, rising, and looking very fair and very pale as she stood in the full morning light. "For some unknown reason—unknown to me—you are not my friend; after all, you do not know me. If I find my life unbearable, I have friends who will help me!"

"Now, Mrs. Drayton, answer me a plain question," and the doctor, rising also, looked at her with a curious expression of mingled distrust and rising interest. "What have you to complain of? Is your husband rough to you. Has he ever done you any injury?"

Poor Margaret!

"He is rough," she said, with hesitation in her voice; "he uses language new to me. But if you can see no strangeness in his manner" . . . . Her voice died away, her hopes had vanished; she had a horrible and undefinable dread—she had seen a wildness in his eyes, which in a less degree she had seen when she had first known him; but our own convictions, unsupported by any facts, are inconclusive to other people—and Dr. Jones, seeing in her a very lovely woman, but one evidently able to deceive, and who did not hesitate to say she had no liberty, when he had seen her alone and out, was steeled against her.

He laid down the law with all the authority of a man who is fully aware of having right on his side.

"Madam, if you have any one tangible grievance—if your husband ever struck you, or ill-treated you in any way—then I should see my way to interfering in your behalf; the law protects you in such a case."

"Yes," Margaret answered, bitterly, "you will interfere, and the law will protect (?) me when I am injured; there is no help for me till the necessity for help has passed away."

She bowed and left him—knowing that her words were useless, and went to try and comfort herself, and *try* and bear her fate without a murmur. Had she not sinned, and against all her convictions, with her eyes open, and fearing this very thing!

"What a very illogical mind she has," said Dr. Jones, as he stalked downstairs, comfortably satisfied that he had been firm, and that her grace, the pathos of her voice, and her great beauty, had alike been disregarded. Justice, without doubt, was on his side—he thought.

But as he stepped on the last step something made him sensible that there might be a little truth in what she said. Though she had told him a deliberate untruth, all might not be false.

'He changed his mind about going home at once, and he went to see Mr. Drayton instead. He found him very quiet, rather depressed, without a trace of excitement in his manner.

Nothing during the interview transpired to give the slightest colour to the wife's dread; and the doctor left, perfectly convinced in his own mind that Mrs. Drayton was quite in the wrong, in more ways than one.

Just as he reached the front door and was full of his own good sense, he heard a sound that startled him, a loud soul-less meaningless laugh, and as the front door shut upon him, pulled by his own hand, a quick, sharp misgiving crossed his mind, and he wished he had seen the man-servant. He had not thought it necessary. But his own convictions soon banished that sudden thought, and the result of his visit was to confirm his views and to give rise to many moral reflections on the way in which glaring faults may be marked by unusual personal advantages.

His wife, who was shrewd and kind-hearted, but who had not that deep estimation for his talents which goes far to make the conjugal relationship happy, was interested in the poor wife and mother living in such a singularly secluded manner. She had only seen her, no one ever being allowed an entrance to the Limes, by Margaret's own wish and consent, when she had found that her husband had a terrible tendency, and which she had no wish to alter had she been able to do so, now the dread had changed.

Mrs. Jones was not a great admirer of her husband's abilities—indeed she had lived to find him peculiarly dull in a great many things; but he was very kind to her, and admired her quickness immensely, so that though the balance was on the wrong side still it was there.

Everything passing in his mind she could generally read pretty clearly, and he did not object to her doing so. He was always rather relieved when she brought her mind to bear upon some perplexity; and, though as far as medical cases went, he was very discreet, there were occasions, of which the present was one, when it was a substantial comfort to have his mode of action approved of by her.

Mrs. Jones was one of the women who have no inclination for prolonged meals, and it was always a trial to her the deliberation and great enjoyment evinced by her husband on these occasions. Some people have no talent for eating, and except for his sake Mrs. Jones would never have gone through that ceremony —to which so many cling—of having a succession of dishes presented one after another, as though you could not have one thing and finish with it, she herself would say; and her luncheon as often as not, consisted of an apple or two which she crunched between her fine white teeth, and a biscuit, the hardness of which tested their capability.

But she was wise enough to understand that a good dinner was really an essential to Mr. Jones, and, without caring about it herself, she threw herself into the subject, and the result was eminently satisfactory.

She bore the prolonged meals, in which her rapid demolition was a standing grievance, with some work on her lap, work which employed her active fingers and left her mind free to apply to any of her husband's interests at the moment.

He had at one time considered this to be "not quite the thing," and had questioned its propriety.

"But it is much better for you, if you could only see it," she had answered. "The work does not prevent my talking, and my dinner does," which argument was unassailable.

Mr. Jones had even come to consider there was great merit in the arrangement, as his wife never hurried him now, or showed by any little feminine indications that the time seemed long.

"I am glad, my dear," he said, when he had arrived at that pleasant stage of affairs when his appetite was partially satisfied, and had yet to be satiated, "I am very glad your acquaintance with Mrs. Drayton went no further."

"Why?"

"I am afraid, my dear (speaking of course in strictest confidence), that she is not quite a straightforward person."

"I hardly know any one I consider quite

straightforward, myself," answered Mrs. Jones calmly. " What has she done ? "

" I think you are making rather a sweeping assertion, my dear," he said, eyeing with a momentary misgiving a roast duck; it looked overdone.

" Never mind my assertions, but tell me what that poor thing has done ? "

" Why do you say that *poor* thing ? I really do not see why she is to be pitied."

" Don't you? well I do. Do you call the life she leads a proper life for a young creature accustomed probably to all the freedom of a country life in Scotland ? I often think of her, and I declare sometimes I should like to force my way into that dismal house, and take her and her child out of it." Mrs. Jones spoke with a vehemence quite surprising to her husband.

" Really, my dear," he said, " the rapid conclusions you arrive at are .... bewildering to my slower mode of thought. You have seen Mrs. Drayton once, and you are ready immediately to credit her with weariness, and the house is a substantial house and very well furnished, and . . . . "

"Do you suppose curtains and carpets can make a woman happy?" asked Mrs. Jones, severely.

"They do something towards it, I think, judging from your own great anxiety upon the subject."

Mr. Jones had some reason for this statement.

"All I have to say is that that poor young creature's heart is broken—yes, broken. I never saw any one so thoroughly and utterly miserable as she is."

Mr. Jones was startled but not convinced.

"I saw her the other day, though not to speak to," Mr. Jones went on. "She went to Skidd's, and I was going in also, but as *you* objected to my being mixed up with her I drew back. A friend of hers happened to go there on business, and she welcomed him, and I saw her face, and its expression has haunted me ever since."

"As you saw her out with your own eyes, you can understand that when she talks of never going out that is not a perfectly true statement," and Mr. Jones, who was longing to have his own slight misgivings set at rest by his wife, took off his spectacles, rubbed imaginary specs off their polished surface, and replaced them.

"One swallow does not make a summer," said Mrs. Jones, with as much contempt in her meaning as she thought befitting. "It is a fact known to every one here that she has only been seen once, and that she is kept exactly as though the Limes was a prison and her husband a jailer."

"Really, my dear, in these days such expressions are quite absurd."

"Their being absurd does not make them false, and I trust that if you can in any way help that poor thing you will."

"If she went out once she can do so again."

"Not at all a certainty; she may have

managed it once, and yet because she did so it may be made impossible for her."

"It strikes me, my dear, that you know more about it all than I imagined," said Dr. Jones, with a sudden perception which for him was really acute.

"I know this, that Mr. Drayton refused her sister shelter on the worst night we have had; that the sisters are orphans devotedly attached to each other; that one sister is ill, and that the other is a prisoner, therefore they cannot meet. They have one or two friends, and the only thing that puzzles me is why the friends do not interfere."

"My dear," and Dr. Jones spoke with great irritation, "how can any one interfere? There is nothing wrong about the man. I saw him to-day. I am not going to proclaim him mad to please his wife or any one else."

"Then she appealed to you?"

"She told me a long story. She wanted more liberty. How can I interfere?"

"And she asked you if her husband was —*that?*"

"Was what?"

"Mad."

"She said something, but as I had seen her out, and she said she could not go out, I did not feel very much inclined to take her view of the question," said the doctor, obstinately.

"Why are you prejudiced against her?"

"Because I saw her meet the *friend* you speak of, and I drew my own conclusions."

"Well, you ought to be ashamed of yourself," said Mrs. Jones, very warmly, "thoroughly ashamed of yourself. As it happens the meeting was a pure accident. Mr. Skidd has been publishing some poetry; he told me about it at first; in fact he showed the first poem to me, and asked me what I thought," said Mrs. Jones, not without a pardonable little glow of satisfaction. "I thought it beautiful. Then the editor of some magazine in London came down and arranged to have all she wrote.

He called by accident and met Mrs. Drayton, and they talked business. How you can put such an ill-natured construction on so simple a thing I cannot make out."

"My dear, I really—putting two and two together—I thought——"

"I shall be afraid of speaking to any one now for fear of your seeing evil in it—Mr. Paul Lyons, for instance—I shall refuse to shake hands with him."

"My dear, I wish you would not go off at a tangent like that. It is a very different thing. You are not in her position; you are not young and beautiful, and . . . . What in the world is the matter now?"

His wife rushed out of the room, and disdained answering him.

In the meantime Jean was bravely facing all her difficulties. Her principal difficulty was that she had a woman to deal with in the shape of a landlady who was what Jean termed a "slithery" creature. When she found that Jean looked after things she was impertinent;

but that had no effect. Jean looked over her head and ignored her altogether.

Then she took to being disobliging, and would neither answer a bell nor give any help. Her next move was to let the kitchen fire out perpetually, and when Jean wanted to heat some soup and get anything hot there was no fire.

She calculated that as Grace was very ill and could not be moved, she would get the best of it in the long run.

But Jean was not a woman who would allow herself to be put out of it without giving her opinion and trying to remedy matters. She had a great contempt for the "wishy-washy" voice and untidy ways of Mrs. Cripps, a woman who lived in a black cap, and knew nothing of any but baker's bread, and could neither make "a scone or even oat-bread, let be bannocks," Jean said to Grace when she was dwelling upon the shortcomings of the house one day.

"I am glad," said Grace, laughing. "I

never cared for oat-bread. I always feel, if I ever try to eat it, that I am eating sand; please do not be offended."

"I'll take no offence where none is meant," said Jean, quietly; "and people are not a' born wi' a good taste."

The landlady tried in vain to speak her high-bred English, and to put herself above her. There are a good many like her that cannot distinguish between provincialism and vulgarity. Jean had a ready tongue, and, though she assured Grace that she kept it well between her teeth, the landlady heard it occasionally, and felt it in all its roughness.

The skirmishes were invariably amusing to Grace, who used to lie in her chair and laugh over the scenes afterwards, and tell them to Paul Lyons, who showed how little any real love had existed for her by the way in which he still came to see her and to hear of Margaret.

She could not help asking herself what she gained in all this unhappiness; she was as badly off as ever. She was still dependent on Mr. Sandford. She was living in a tiny lodging. She disliked the doctor, and never would see him if she could help it, and the sister, who had all their lives been her one great stay and support, had no liberty to come and see her.

She had planned her life so differently, and it came vividly before her. How proud she had always been of the cleverness, which tested at length, had failed in every particular. But once she rallied, hers was not at all the nature to dwell upon unpleasant things. The first day she went out she drove to the Limes, taking Jean with her, and they asked for Mrs. Drayton.

"Mrs. Drayton is out," said the man-servant, who did not dare say otherwise.

"Hoot! man," said Jean, "you need not tell me that. Why, Mrs. Drayton is never out."

"Shut that door immediately," called out an angry voice, and Mr. Drayton, looking very haggard and wild, came to the door.

"My sister! I want to see my sister," and Grace held out her hands imploringly.

Mr. Drayton came down the steps and looked at her; then he made a perfectly diabolical face, burst into a roar of laughter, and slammed the door in her face.

Grace, weak and terrified, clung to Jean as they went home. "What shall we do? What shall we do?" she sobbed. "Oh, Jean! that man is mad, and she, my poor Margaret, is in his power!"

"Whist, my dear bairn," said Jean, who was nigh upon tears herself. "Whist! I think we will be guided," she said, reverently, and she sat silent for a few minutes. "I doubt we will have to speak to the police," she added, as that brilliant idea came to console her.

Grace wrote a letter to Mrs. Dorriman that night, in which she told her all she knew, all she feared, for the first time; she expressed her gratitude for all the kindness she had received; for the first time she acknowledged that she was to blame, and she asked to express something of her feeling to Mr. Sandford.

This done she felt more happy than she had done lately, and rose next day trusting that in some way her sister's freedom would be brought about.

Mr. Lyons called early, and was delighted to receive her confidence. Might he go and call? Surely there could be no harm, he asked, anxiously; it might save time.

"It would only make matters worse for my sister," Grace said, "and you would do no good."

"But it will show that she—that your sister —has friends near her."

"That very fact might rouse him to more violence, and my sister would suffer."

"I might go and call on *him*. I do not believe he would be violent if I asked for him. I am afraid he knows me, otherwise I might take some circulars and call upon him about business."

"As if you know anything about business."

"I assure you I have been very hard at work lately. I have gone into the question of employment very seriously."

"I doubt your having done anything seriously," laughed Grace.

"That is rather hard on a fellow, when a fellow has really tried."

"Come, Mr. Lyons, what have you tried?"

"I have offered myself as an agent to begin with. Agency is a very good thing. You spend no money yourself, and other people's money sticks to your fingers; it is really a very simple thing."

"And what are you agent for, may I ask?"

"Oh! the appointment is not confirmed, but I think I am on the high road to it. It does not much matter what it is as long as you can get people to buy. I have at this moment two things before me, of which I have really a very fair chance."

"Have you?"

"Are you sufficiently interested, Miss Rivers, to hear what they are?"

"I am doing my best to show my interest by listening to you with both my ears."

"Ah! but you are *not* giving me your undivided attention. You are knitting, and just now I quite distinctly heard you count five. A fellow cannot talk of his prospects to a girl while she counts five," Mr. Lyons said, in a tone of disgust, and looking round the room appealing to an imaginary audience.

"I will not count again—only just this once. I have made a mistake already;" and Grace wrinkled her forehead and became absorbed in her work for a few moments.

"Miss Rivers, will you really let a fellow talk to you? life and death does not hang upon a few stitches more or less."

"No, but a sock does; and dear Mrs. Dorriman took such pains to teach me to make one."

"You are always knitting," the young man said, discontentedly.

"No; only when I feel very good," she answered, gravely; "then I knit all kinds of things into my sock."

"What sort of things—colours? that thing looks all the same colour to me."

"Oh, I do not mean material things, but sorrow and penitence—and the bitterest repentance," she added the last words in a lower tone, and her eyes were concealed under lowered lids; then she sighed.

Mr. Lyons sighed also, he had a very good idea what she referred to.

"To return to your wishes," said Grace, laughing a little, to carry off a feeling of awkwardness at having shown emotion; "what do you wish to tell me?"

"It—it sounds a little frivolous now. I only wanted to say I have tried to get into every agency you can think of. I have gone steadily down the alphabet and picked out everything you can think of. It is quite astonishing how many things there are to be canvassed for. I did the W's yesterday, and the X's and Y's to-day. I took the W's out of their turn because of wine; there are such an enormous number of firms who sell or want to sell *the* only drinkable wine; and it is a subject I know a little about."

"And you got nothing?"

"Considerably less than nothing. One question was asked—introductions—references, and, as I had never thought of an introduction, and could refer to no one as to my ability—I was bowed out. I met with civility, I will say; I had on my best coat, and that tells," he said, in a tone of satisfaction.

"Perhaps something may turn up," Grace answered brightly.

"I hope so; you see, I never could do much more than sign my name—my handwriting is simply abominable. It has happened to me to have my address and signature cut out of my own letter and pasted on as the only way of solving the problem of where I lived, and then it sometimes wandered about a good deal before it reached me;" and he laughed at the recollection. Grace laughed with him.

"But what is your plan as regards Margaret,

my poor darling sister?" she asked, and her countenance changed.

"If I was agent to something in which Mr. Drayton was interested I could ask to see him on business, and if I could only get a recommendation or introduction to him all would be easy; once in the house I am not afraid." The young man drew up his head and looked quite ready for anything that might happen.

Grace clasped her hands. "I think it is a very good plan," she exclaimed, "and I can help you a little myself. What do you call a manufactory that turns out horrible smells, and kills trees and plants and things"

"Artificial manures?" he said, pulling a list out of his pocket and referring to it.

"Oh, dear no," said Grace, impatiently, "it makes all the trees look like skeletons. Who ever heard of manure killing anything? it makes them grow."

"I spoke without thinking, only remembering that that made an appalling smell, quite enough to kill everything."

"Well, think, with all your might, or, still better, think, and give me your list—and if I saw the name I should know it—and you can think in the meantime," said Grace, speaking very quickly.

"I have it!" she exclaimed, joyfully pointing with her finger to it and holding out the paper to him. "Chemical works! now do not forget, chemical, chemical, chemical—say it over and over again, for fear of forgetting it. Well, Mr. Lyons, at Renton there is a huge large chemical work, and Mr. Drayton used to go there constantly. I remember his saying one day that he had invested money—a quantity of money—in these things."

"That will do then," he said. "I will boldly ask for Mr. Drayton to-morrow morning, and ask if he is still interested in the Renton chemical works. You will see, all will go well."

"I pray that it may. I shall write a long letter to my poor darling and entreat her to tell me exactly the state of the case. She has so much cleverness that I *cannot* understand her not coming to see me. She must have some difficulty to contend with we know nothing of."

"Ask her to suggest some plan herself, if she requires help of any kind," said young Lyons.

"Yes, only she is so horribly conscientious, she may make difficulties. Her spirit seems so broken."

"Hearing that man laugh is quite enough to make one wish never to laugh again. However, now that I have something definite to do I feel happier. Oh! if all only goes well.

"I hope Lady Lyons is not uneasy about your being so much away."

"No, she is quite accustomed to my erratic movements. Good-bye, and if . . . . "

He stopped, turned very red, and went swiftly out of her presence.

CHAPTER X.

MARGARET found the days pass on with a monotony which was very terrible to her. At times her husband joined her at dinner, but she never knew when to expect him. Sometimes he came into the nursery, when he would sit watching her and the child, in whom her love (starved in every other direction) centred so completely.

She learned to be horribly afraid of him. She could not understand how the doctor could reconcile it to his conscience to speak of him as sane; there was such a wildness in his eyes, and a vagueness in his laughter, which made her shiver with fright.

She forgot the great cunning that forms so great a feature in some kind of insanity, and, always viewing him with nervous eyes, she heard him speak rationally at times without noticing it, because her mind was always on the stretch, and mental anxiety is apt to distort everything. He had generally, however, fits of silence when she was only conscious of his eyes gleaming at her from under the shaggy eyebrows, and these prolonged periods of silence were far, far more acceptable to her than his terrible laugh. Each day she prayed with all her soul for health and strength—she tried, poor child, to do her duty, and, sometimes full of pity for his evident supreme unhappiness, she tried to talk to him and to interest him in their child. He watched her unceasingly. In the garden, where now spring flowers were coming out, where the birds began to chirp and twitter, and where the trees showed green, and another spring had come to gladden the earth.

It brought no rejoicing to her heart, because there must be a responsive chord somewhere, and to enter into the fair happiness of spring the pulses must be able to beat a little quickly, and some sympathy between the great new birth of the year and the soul must be possible. The cheerfulness of outside nature seemed almost a mockery to her—just as the overflowing mirth of a casual acquaintance jars upon one in sorrow.

Her writing began to be noticed, and at times her nurse, who had been unsympathetic and suspicious at first, but who had grown to love her, managed to bring her carefully-written letters from Grace, and news from the outside world, though Margaret seldom dared to ask her to make the attempt, she was so afraid that this one human being in whom she had begun to have trust might be taken from her. She dreaded night because, though locked in with her child, the nurse sleeping in an adjoining room, she would often wake in a paroxysm of terror, thinking that in some way her husband had gained an entrance to her room, and that he was threatening her and her child.

She was walking in the garden with her sorrowful thoughts, watching her little darling, when the front door-bell rang loudly, a sound so seldom heard as to be startling to her.

Mr. Drayton, who used to sit in a room off the front hall, of which the window commanded the garden, went as usual into the hall to see that no one went out or came in, and heard his own name mentioned by a peremptory and loud-voiced man, who demanded instant admission, to see him on urgent business.

"Tell him I have done with business, I refuse to see him."

"But you will be extremely sorry if you do not see me," said the stranger in a still louder tone. "You thought you had made a mess of those chemical work shares, but you have been a far, far cleverer man than we gave you credit for. Those shares Mr. Sandford laughed at . . . ."

"Come in here, come in here," said Mr. Drayton, rubbing his hands with glee. "So I was right, and that old fool was wrong, hah! hah! hah!" and he laughed uproariously.

The stranger walked into the small room;

he could hardly believe, he said, that Mr. Drayton's acute intelligence had been laughed at. What shares had he had in those works; what papers had he to show? Perhaps that was a matter of no moment. If the shares had been sold .... why it was a misfortune, unless he could buy them back before the discovery, the great discovery, was made known.

"What discovery?" asked Mr. Drayton, in a moment suspicious.

"That you were right and every one else wrong."

"How has that discovery been made?"

"By experiment."

"Yes; but who made the experiment?"

The stranger leaned forward and said in a low voice, "You remember your manager, the man who left you?"

"Remember him! You do not mean to say he is in the thick of this—the scoundrel, the—the rascal." Then suspicion came to him again.

"What interest in all this have you?" he asked, very angrily, and glaring at the stranger fiercely.

"Interest? you do not suppose I have come to you for nothing; that would be rather a good joke," and he laughed heartily.

"Of course not, of course not. But from what motive? No one does anything for nothing," and Mr. Drayton put on an air of wisdom, in which cunning was very visible.

"I should think not, indeed; and I am not working for nothing, I can tell you. In the first place, a friend of mine has been most abominably treated — shockingly, shamefully treated!"

"By whom?"

"By some one connected with these works" (and I am sure that is true, said Paul Lyons to himself, since he, this man, has been connected with them).

"Can't you tell his name?"

"No, I can't, it would spoil all my plans if I did" (and so it would, he thought).

"I do not believe in disinterested friendships."

"Nor do I; but I intend having a reward."

"From me, I suppose," and Mr. Drayton laughed again.

"From you—and from some one else. If my ideas are correct—you would not grudge me a good percentage, eh?"

"What do you call a good percentage?"

"Well, I want half; I want fifty per cent."

"Fifty per cent.! nonsense, absolute nonsense."

"You have no right to say 'nonsense'; and I think I am wasting my time" (which is also true, it is quite wonderful how I have been able to speak the truth to-day), and Paul Lyons felt a glow of satisfaction at this reflection.

"I don't know what you're driving at;" and Mr. Drayton looked so furiously at him that Paul Lyons thought if he ever favoured Margaret with such a glance it was enough to give her a fit.

"I am driving at nothing," he said, with a

very good show of anger. "I don't pretend that I shan't be abominably annoyed if you do not go into this matter, because I see my way to making some money, but it seems to me that you have no papers to show me, and that you do not understand this matter very much; I believe I had better go—time, as far as I am concerned, is too precious to waste."

He rose and made a movement towards the door. Mr Drayton put his hand to his forehead; he felt confused; he never now could follow a thought for any time, but his cunning made him anxious to conceal this.

"You can stop," he said, speaking a little thickly, and more slowly. "I have some papers upstairs."

"Let your servant fetch them."

"No; certainly not. I will go myself."

He left the room, and Paul threw up the window, flung out a packet, and closed it again.

Margaret saw the packet fall, but she also saw her husband at the upstairs window;

therefore, to the young man's disappointment, she continued walking along, holding her little one's hand, and took no notice.

Mr. Drayton returned, holding some papers in his hands.

"What did you open the window for?" he asked, and Paul saw that his suspicions were again aroused.

"Open the window!" he answered, with great presence of mind. "My dear Mr. Drayton, if you said that to any one else you would be accused of having delusions!"

Mr. Drayton glared at him, and said no more. Paul took the papers and glanced them over; they were lists in Mr. Drayton's own hand-writing; and lists no sane man would have written. Here and there a number put down, and a long rambling note about some one supposed to have injured him; remarks about a man who took various shapes, and who made fiendish faces at him; and things of that sort.

Paul Lyons was not experienced in cases of

the kind; this man, whom he felt to be insane (though evidently having lucid intervals), was a new revelation to him; but his heart beat violently. He had seen poor Margaret's face, and had recognised that she was pining under the influence of confinement, and probably terrors; and he felt sure that in his hand he held proofs that must be listened to—that he had that now in his possession which must ensure her freedom.

He affected to hunt for papers in his own pockets, and said carelessly, as he crammed the papers into the breast-pocket of his coat, "I will look these over and compare them with what I have at home. Shall I find you at home to-morrow, Mr. Drayton?"

There was no answer, and looking up at him he saw that he was looking out of the window with a face full of malignancy—there was something horrible in his expression as he watched poor Margaret, who had seen the packet, and who had not dared to lift it yet. She had passed close to it once or twice, and had pushed it under a bush with a careless kick. Taken aback by this sign of animosity towards Margaret, Paul Lyons did not know what to do.

He was afraid of making things worse for her, and yet he could not bear going without giving and receiving a sign from her.

"Is that not your wife?" he asked suddenly. "Will you not introduce me to her?"

"Quite impossible, sir — quite impossible. My wife is not all there; she is mad, poor thing, very mad."

"Is she indeed? Well, all the same I should like to speak to her, I should like to make sure that this is not another of your . . . ." He stopped short.

"Another of my ——! Finish, pray finish, my dear sir;" and Mr. Drayton spoke in a tone of suppressed fury.

"Delusions," said the young man, calmly, trying to remember all the various theories about subduing a madman by the expression of the eye, and staring at him hard, conscious all the time of failure.

With sudden fury Mr. Drayton turned upon him, "I believe you to be an impostor, an impostor, sir, do you hear? and you have come here to do me an injury;" he moved towards him threateningly.

"Sir," answered Paul, understanding directly that it was no moment for trifling, "I shall go and I shall tell all the world that Mr. Sandford is right; you understand nothing of business; you are abusive—and, in short, no one can make anything of you."

As he spoke Mr. Drayton nearly grasped him, but he had youth and activity on his side, and he slipped away from him and stood by the window, having thrown down all the chairs.

"Now, sir," he said, "I intend seeing for myself if Mrs. Drayton is mad." Before Mr. Drayton could get round the obstructions he had opened the window, which was not many feet from the ground, and alighted on the lawn close to where Margaret, with deadly anxiety lest the packet should never come into her possession, paced to and fro—she had her child still with her.

"Your husband is mad," said Paul in a hurried whisper, "I hold proofs, and you will be rescued." He stooped and picked up the child, anxious to try and pacify Mr. Drayton now he had spoken those few words to poor Margaret, and forgetting that the child, unaccustomed to any strangers, might be frightened.

The little one, who had been unusually fretful all the morning, which was the reason Margaret tried to amuse it in the fresh air for a longer time than usual, uttered the most piercing shrieks, and just as Mr. Drayton came up to them almost foaming at the mouth. She struggled, and kicked, and clutched hold of the wig, which had made Paul Lyons unrecognisable, even to Margaret, and tore it off, revealing his curly hair.

A perfect roar burst from Mr. Drayton.

Margaret, soothing her child in her arms, watched with terror-stricken eyes the terrible struggle that then ensued. The one man, heavier and stronger with rage, and the other, lithe and pliable, keeping him at times at bay, and at others closing with his adversary. As they neared the little side door, Margaret saw it open slowly, and saw the manservant there.

In a moment she seized the packet and rushed into the house, and upstairs, never taking breath till the doors were locked behind her, and that she was safe in her room with the child, from whence she could see the road.

The struggle went on and Paul was nearly overpowered, when the servant interfered, and, catching hold of Mr. Drayton's uplifted arm, told Paul to go.

"I will go if you will promise to protect Mrs. Drayton from this madman till help come to her," he gasped, bruised and breathless, but feeling that it had not all been a failure since he had given her hope.

"She won't hurt," said the man, "but I'm

not going to stop. I would not stay with him," he said, contemptuously, "not for double the money."

"But you will stay till some one comes, will you not?" Paul asked, more afraid than ever.

"He'll have to look sharp then," said the man. "I've told the doctor my mind, and that its a case of asylum, but he did not choose, he does not choose, to believe me, and I am not going to stay here to be murdered, I can tell you. It's two men's work to look after him, and he's that cunning he speaks the doctor fair when he comes, and the doctor's a fool besides."

Paul lost no time—he rushed out of the house and made his way to an hotel, where he tried to remove all signs of the frightful struggle he had just had, and to sally forth before his old spruce self.

What ought to be his first step? He must lose no time—leaving Margaret even for a day in the power of that madman was horrible to him.

Even Grace was not thought of; clutching his papers, he went to the magistrate who presided over the district court and sent in his card and asked for an interview. At first he was received with natural suspicion, his face was swollen and he looked altogether as though he had been mixed up in a fray, though his dress was so carefully arranged—but the merit of reality was there, and he sketched in glowing colours poor Margaret's position and the treatment he had received, and what he feared for her, in simple language free from exaggeration.

The magistrate consulted his clerk and sundry authorities with a deliberation truly maddening.

"I am searching for a precedent," he said, looking up at young Lyons, who was almost stamping with impatience.

He turned over leaves, backwards and forwards, and read and re-read passages pointed out to him by the clerk. Then he looked up, a bright idea having dawned upon him, and, keeping his first finger on a particular line, said :

"Are you the lady's nearest male relation?"

"No, I am not. Her only male relation is very ill in Scotland."

"Are you any relation of hers?"

"No; I am her friend."

"My *dear* sir," said the magistrate, "why take up my time in this way? You have no right to interfere—there is no precedent for such a thing, no precedent at all," and he got up and stood leaning his knuckles on the table and looking at Paul Lyons as though his ignorance of the law was almost worthy of compassion.

"Will you advise me, sir? What am I to do? Can you not tell me how I must set to work? Surely your experience can help me."

"No, sir; I really cannot take the responsibility of doing this—the lady's nearest relations must take the matter up. You had better not interfere."

"And if the lady has no relations?"

"That, sir, is a position—hem - the law never contemplated such a position. I really must beg you to withdraw now, you are taking up the time of the (he was going to say court but he corrected himself)—you are taking up my time, sir."

With hidden rage, poor Paul left him, and found himself in the street. What was the right thing to do? How could he help her?

He went to see Grace to consult with her; she cried and then laughed, and go t quite hysterical.

"Oh! you foolish boy, I am her nearest relation, and I will send for the doctor; they sent him to me, but I got rid of him, I disliked him so much. We will have him here, and I will see if I cannot talk him into helping us."

She wrote a note and sent it off, and Paul, who by this time knew he had had no food for a long time, went off to his hotel, promising to be back again to meet the doctor and tell him the state of matters.

The picture he had drawn of Mr. Drayton's

violence filled Grace with anxiety. She moved about restlessly, filling up the time by trying various occupations and throwing each aside one after another.

Jean, coming to see if she wanted anything, found her in a fever, and when she heard all was nearly "demented," to use her own expression. She talked and remonstrated and suggested all in a breath. The police, that would be a help.

When Mr. Lyons returned, this idea was given to him by Grace, and he was inclined to think it might help. He went off to find the superintendent, and was met by fresh difficulties.

The superintendent asked what he was afraid of, and laughed at the idea of his being called upon to protect a lady who had made no complaint. Urged by Paul at length he said,

"I will tell the man on that beat to look out, and if he hears screams ——"

"He will of course at once get admittance," said Paul, eagerly, horrified to hear his own fears put into actual words.

The superintendent smiled—a superior smile,

"No, sir," he must not enter any man's house unless he is *called* in, it would be breaking the law."

"Then he must wait till murder is committed before interfering.".

"Well, you see, sir, little rows and things cannot be interfered with unless one of the parties asks for help."

"It seems to me" said Paul, driven nearly to despair, "that the laws all round want a good deal of amendment."

"Perhaps so, sir, I'm sure I cannot say, but I have to see that my men do their duty, and that they do not exceed it."

Paul went back to tell Grace that the man on the beat was to be at hand, and it did not occur to her fortunately to ask what good being at hand would do for Margaret. But she had found out through the landlady that if two doctors declared Mr. Drayton to be mad, they could get a magistrate's order and have him put under restraint.

"After all, you have done a great deal more than I have done; I have wasted my day, and done nothing," said poor Paul, who was fairly tired out. Grace did not contradict him; so far from thinking she had done much she felt as though all the real effort, all the great trial, had yet to come.

She awaited with impatience the arrival of the doctor, turning over in her own mind after her usual fashion what she should say and how she should say it.

On his arrival he was surprised to find her sitting up when he had imagined her very ill; he stopped short, and gazed at her a little helplessly—what did she want with him?

As may be remembered, he had not been accustomed to much beauty, and was always on his guard against being influenced by it in an undue manner.

Grace was not so beautiful as Margaret, but she was not like the ordinary women he had seen; he had got into a groove of very middle-aged ladies, and, seeing them in private, saw them bereft of those adornments which concealed the ravages of time from the outside world.

Grace with her rippling hair tumbling over her shoulders, a heightened colour and sparkling eyes, prejudiced him directly.

So handsome a young woman must be certainly very wicked. Doctor Jones is not the only person in the world who imagines that goodness and plainness walk hand in hand. He prepared from the first therefore to act on the defensive, and his tone, asking, "You wished to see me, madam," was distinctly aggressive, and Grace, sensitive and anxious, recognized the tone and felt that at the outset she was met with a difficulty.

"Doctor Jones, you have seen and you know my sister, Mrs. Drayton."

"I have seen her; I cannot say that I *know* her; one cannot know a person just by seeing them for a moment or two."

"Well," said Grace, a little impatiently, "you know her husband, Mr. Drayton?"

"Slightly; yes, slightly, I do know him."

"Do you know that he is—mad?"

"No, I know nothing of the kind. Who says so, Miss Rivers?"

"I *know* it," said Grace, "and something must be done immediately!" She spoke with rising excitement.

"I cannot understand what you're driving at."

"Doctor Jones, a friend of ours went there to-day; he saw Mr. Drayton, and he told me if something was not done immediately he was quite quite certain that my sister will suffer. I am afraid for her poor child."

"Is she afraid for herself?" he asked, with a disagreeable smile.

"How can I tell?" said Grace, angrily; "he does not allow her to move without him; she is a very prisoner in that terrible house, she cannot come and see me; she escaped once and he has taken means to prevent her ever coming again. He does not allow her to go to church or to see a single soul. He must be mad, he is mad!"

"If I were Mr. Drayton and had a wife like your sister I would do the same, Miss Rivers."

"What do you mean?" she cried, passionately.

"Miss Rivers, your sister did not even allow to me that she had been out once. I saw her; I saw her meet her —— I *know* it was her lover, in a shop."

Grace stared at him for a moment, and then she laughed wildly and hysterically.

"Poor Paul!" she said; "imagine, only imagine, being taken for Margaret's lover!"

Doctor Jones rose; he was exceedingly affronted.

"You and your sister, madam, must find a less honest man to help you carry out your wicked plans against poor Mr. Drayton's happiness. I am incorruptible!" and, with his head well in the air and a strong sense of virtuous resistance to beauty and blandishments, he prepared to go.

"Doctor Jones," said Grace, her burst of

laughter over, " you have said a very wicked and a very ridiculous thing, but you had better go away. After your fancying anything wrong about Margaret I cannot bear seeing you. Why, the only excuse for you is, that you are probably as mad as Mr. Drayton."

"Madam, you may throw off the mask now and be impertinent, but nothing you say will move me. I am not going to declare a man mad when I believe him to be sane, to suit you or any one else."

"It does not in the least matter," said Grace, coolly, and speaking from the inspiration of the moment, "for the man whom I shall probably marry if I get strong, the man you imagine to be my sister's lover, will be here soon, and he will most likely bring Sir Augustus Jermyn down with him. I have great faith in *him*, and Sir Augustus will probably prefer naming the second medical man himself."

Doctor Jones was very much taken aback. It was hard that being an honest man should prevent his being thrown with so eminent a man.

"I—I should have no objection to meeting Sir Augustus and giving him my opinion. I should feel proud to assist him in forming a judgment."

"I have no doubt of it," said Grace, sarcastically, "but nothing will induce me now to mention your name to Sir Augustus. You have too completely prejudged and misjudged my dearest sister. You see her meet a friend, a friend much attached to us both, and jump immediately to iniquitous conclusions. Leave me! I never will forgive you, and if anything happens to my sister on you will the whole responsibility fall."

Doctor Jones retired, endeavouring to comfort himself with the reflection that he had acted purely from a sense of right. But that small, still voice—that voice that may be listened to or not but is always there—convicted him. He knew that because he thought Margaret in the wrong he had been resolved not to agree with her. He got positively hot with sudden tremor. What if Sir Augustus came, and found the man really mad! His opinion would henceforth be valueless, and, just as he thought this, the remembrance of Mr. Drayton's laugh was most uncomfortably present to him.

He said nothing to his wife of this; he must not lower himself in her opinion at any rate.

When he left the room Grace began to try and think if Paul had ever spoken of meeting Margaret. By degrees then it all came to her. Sir Albert Gerald must have met her, and that reptile of a doctor had seen them speak to each other. At the time she had forgotten this.

How difficult life was to her just now, and the fears for Margaret came to her in fuller force than ever.

Jean came into the room, her big Bible under her arm, her eyes shining with a look of content and peace. She noticed Grace's troubled expression, and she stroked her long hair.

"My bairn," she said, "it's a troublous world at times I know."

"It is all sent for the best," said Grace, giving utterance to the platitude nearest her lips at the moment

"Oh! do not say that. You must na say that. We make evil to ourselves, God does *not* send it."

"He allows it," murmured Grace.

"Bairn, I ask you, and answer from your own conscience: Who brought all this weary trouble upon us?"

She stood like an inspired sybil, her brown face and homely features lighted by a Divine truth, and Grace, looking up, conscience-stricken, could only answer the truth, slowly and solemnly,

"It was I, Jean, I myself."

END OF VOL. II.

Westminster: Printed by Nichols and Sons, 25, Parliament Street.

www.ingramcontent.com/pod-product-compliance
Lightning Source LLC
Chambersburg PA
CBHW030815230426
43667CB00008B/1222